FINANCIAL RECOVERY PLANS IN THE NH

CW00507055

Foreword

Financial recovery plans (FRPs) are now an integral part of the financial planning process in most NHS organisations and continual improvement in financial performance is expected from all. There is no 'one size fits all' approach to developing a recovery plan. However, there are a number of generic issues that all organisations are likely to think through. This guide focuses on these common areas and provides some practical pointers drawn from real life examples that may help at each stage of the process. This guide will also help organisations as they seek to deliver continual improvement in their financial performance, thereby leading to better services for patients.

In particular, the guide looks at how organisations:

- Establish their baseline position
- Communicate and involve all those affected by the FRP
- Set their FRP in context, establish aims and agree milestones
- Formulate a practical strategy that delivers cost improvement measures and manages risk.

There is also a section that sets out tips that should help your FRP to be a success. The guide draws on examples from across England and develops some of the ideas discussed at recent HFMA seminars on this subject. Although the guide is based on the situation in England, the principles that underpin financial recovery plans are equally relevant across the whole of the UK.

We trust that you will find this guide of use as you develop your financial recovery plans. If you have any comments, please let us know at: technical.support@hfma.org.uk

Andy Leary
Chairman
HFMA Financial Management and Research Committee

Acknowledgments

This guide has been produced under the guidance and direction of the HFMA's Financial Management and Research Committee. The HFMA is grateful to the committee's members for their help and support and to all those organisations that allowed us to reproduce material from their recovery plans.

Particular thanks are due to Barry Elliot and Rob Yeomans from Surrey and Sussex Strategic Health Authority - it was their approach to financial recovery and their willingness to share what they had developed with others that inspired the production of this guide. We are also grateful to Jane Cole from Hampshire and Isle of Wight Strategic Health Authority, Phil Richards from Hinchingbrooke Health Care NHS Trust, Tony Waite from Mid Yorkshire Hospitals NHS Trust and Nick Webb from Shropshire PCT for their contributions.

The members of the HFMA's Financial Management and Research Committee are:

Andy Leary (Chairman)
Jane Cole
Steve Elliot
Anna Green
Melanie Kay
Cathy Kennedy
Emma Knowles
Amanda Munro
Sheenagh Powell
Karl Simkins
Paul Taylor
Roger Tester
Robert White
Keith Wood
Janet Wood

1 Chapter One

What are Financial Recovery Plans?

Financial recovery plans (FRPs) have become an integral part of the financial planning process in many NHS organisations and continual improvement in financial performance is required from all. This is reflected in the Department of Health's guide Delivering Excellence in Financial Governance which states that 'the need to achieve financial duties should be built into the financial plan with recovery plans incorporated where these are required'.

The Department also issues detailed guidance on breakeven duty and provisions in its finance manuals and circulars. The key circular for NHS Trusts is HSC 1999/146 Guidance to Health Authorities and NHS Trusts on Break-Even Duty; Provisions and Accumulated Deficits. This is available via the HSC pages of the Department of Health's website:
http://www.dh.gov.uk/PublicationsAndStatistics/LettersAndCirculars/HealthServiceCirculars/fs/en

For PCTs guidance in relation to resource limits and financial balance is available from:
http://www.dh.gov.uk/PolicyAndGuidance/OrganisationPolicy/PrimaryCare/PrimaryCareTrusts/fs/en

The manuals for all NHS bodies can be found at
http://www.info.doh.gov.uk/doh/finman.nsf/

In relation to recovery plans, the manual for NHS trusts is an essential source of reference. Although this is written with NHS trusts in mind it is also relevant to PCTs. What follows is taken from the 'detailed guidance' section:

Agreed Recovery Plans

Where an NHS Trust is recovering a cumulative deficit position, the NHS Trust will be required to produce and agree with its host SHA a robust recovery plan. This recovery plan should recover the deficit position over the shortest possible period. Both the NHS Trust and the host SHA will position over the shortest possible period. Both the NHS Trust and the host SHA will also need to agree how the deficit can be cash managed in the interim without breaching the public sector payments policy (now the Better Practice Payment Code).

The process for formally agreeing plans with NHS Trusts recovering cumulative deficits is left to the discretion of individual host SHA. But whatever process is adopted will need to take account of the scale of deficit being recovered and the service implications of proposed plans to achieve financial recovery. There is also a minimum requirement for content of an agreed financial recovery plan.

Appendix 2 (reproduced below) gives details of the minimum information required in a financial recovery plan.

Key stakeholders should be involved from the outset in the production of any recovery plan. The unconditional agreement of these key stakeholders should be gained to the content, detail and deliverability of the recovery plan. Key stakeholders will include the relevant SHAs; key commissioners; and members of the NHS Trust's Board who are critically involved in the delivery of the recovery plan. Through this process the recovery plan can be considered in the context of the local health economy rather than purely as the NHS Trust's problem; and the end product jointly owned by all stakeholders.

The recovery plan must have the explicit support of all key commissioner(s) with a clear sign up to any service and/or financial consequences associated with the recovery plan.

Appendix 2: essential elements of a FRP

1. An outline of the background/cause of the financial problems so as to provide confidence that the remedies proposed are both appropriate and will be effective in restoring financial balance. The nature/cause of the financial problem may include:

- Financial control issues

- Configuration issues (service and/or organisational)
- Activity and cost pressures
- General management issues
- The financial positions of commissioners.

2. The extent of the financial problem:

- A clear quantification of the size of the financial problem
- The identification of any assumptions in arriving at the above
- An analysis of the problem over the various elements giving rise to the nature/cause of the problem (as 1 above)
- An assessment of the underlying financial position i.e. does the problem relate to the current or prior years? Is it recurring or non recurring?
- An assessment of the current and future trend of the problem i.e. has the problem stabilised or is it growing/reducing.

3. A description of any measures/action taken to date to address the financial problem. This should include an assessment of the effect of any measures/action taken, for example:

- Savings plans, including the effect upon service levels, services generally, organisational changes, human resources etc
- Securing additional funds.

4. A description of the measures planned (and agreed) to address the financial problem in order to restore the NHS Trust to a balanced financial position (with key milestones) on a recurring basis and, where appropriate, to effect the recovery of prior year deficits, including:

- Detailed savings plans
- Securing additional funds
- Service impact including service levels, waiting lists/times, reconfigurations
- Organisational impact, including human resources, reconfigurations.

The above must be quantified and profiled by year (and preferably quarterly within year).

5. An assessment of the risks associated with the delivery of the recovery plan, including:

- An assessment of the risks for each element of the recovery plan, including sensitivity and materiality
- Details of the contingency measures in place should any of the risks materialise.

6. An assessment of the cash impact of the financial problem, including:

- The NHS Trust's ability to meet its EFL
- How any in year cash deficit will be managed in the short term
- The restoration of cash and a "healthy" balance sheet in the medium term
- The impact on working capital, restrictions on capital expenditure, sale of fixed assets etc
- Details of any brokerage agreed and the repayment requirements

The above must be quantified and profiled by year (and preferably quarterly within year).

7. Financial proforma must be provided in support of the recovery plan and must:

- Include an I&E account, balance sheet, EFL statement and a cash flow statement
- Cover at least the period of recovery
- Demonstrate that the NHS Trust is returned to underlying financial balance by the end of the recovery period
- Show that the NHS Trust is returned to a healthy cash position/balance sheet by the end of the recovery period (or earlier).

8. A description of the control environment by which progress against the recovery will be monitored, including:

- Written evidence of support from commissioner(s) and SHA approval
- Clear milestones against which the implementation of the recovery plan will be measured and where intervention will be necessary

- Details of performance management meetings (such as steering groups) involving the SHA, commissioner(s) and the NHS Trust
- Nature and frequency of Board level monitoring within the NHS Trust.

Provided an organisation has an effective approach to financial management generally and to financial planning and monitoring in particular, FRPs should be a natural process. This view is consistent with the Audit Commission's conclusions in its publication Achieving First-class Financial Management in the NHS. This emphasises that 'good financial management arrangements are essential if NHS bodies are to meet their objectives and deliver effective healthcare to patients' and points out that 'Having good financial management arrangements should also help managers to identify where things are going wrong and to respond to them in both the short and the medium term'.

In practice, FRPs are the formal expression of how an organisation plans to deal with a 'cumulative deficit position'. The aim of a FRP is to demonstrate a well structured, well planned and practical way forward that will achieve financial stability and sustainability. Out of context, this may sound fairly straightforward. However, given the critical importance of financial stability to service planning and delivery, the fact that there is a statutory duty to break even and the general political environment within which health bodies operate, FRPs are rarely straightforward in practice. They also absorb considerable managerial effort and can cause anxiety for all involved, particularly when the problems faced are substantial and have an impact on services.

It is essential to bear in mind that achieving financial balance is a **statutory** duty. Section 10 (1) of the NHS and Community Care Act 1990 states that 'Every trust shall ensure that its revenue is not less than sufficient, taking one financial year with another[1], to meet outgoings properly chargeable to revenue account'. This is known as the 'break-even duty'. PCTs are required to keep expenditure within their resource limit each year. There is also a Department of Health 'administrative duty' resulting from resource accounting and budgeting that requires NHS bodies to achieve break even each and every year. These duties are of paramount importance - under no circumstances should they be viewed as optional.

---

[1] One year with another is taken to mean over a three or five year rolling period.

It is also important to remember that external auditors have a specific duty to 'consider whether NHS bodies have put in place adequate arrangements to ensure that their financial standing is soundly based'[2]. If auditors have concerns about financial standing they will raise them directly with the board and if satisfactory action is not taken a public interest report (PIR) may be issued. Detailed guidance on auditors' reporting options in relation to concerns about financial standing and performance - including board letters, PIRs and section 19 referrals - are set out in the Audit Commission's September 2004 publication 'Audit Reporting of NHS Financial Performance'. This includes a helpful decision tree, which is reproduced below. The full report is available on the Audit Commission's website: www.audit-commission.gov.uk

Although the ultimate aim of each FRP is the same (to recover a deficit), they can also help organisations to deliver continual improvement in financial performance. The detail and approach followed will depend on an organisation's circumstances and the scale of the problem faced. There is no single 'right' way of developing a FRP. Similarly, the reasons why organisations need to develop FRPs are many and varied: the next section looks at some of the reasons why deficits have arisen.

---

[2]Code of Audit Practice, Audit Commission www.audit-commission.gov.uk

Source: Audit Reporting of NHS Financial Performance, Audit Commission, 2004.

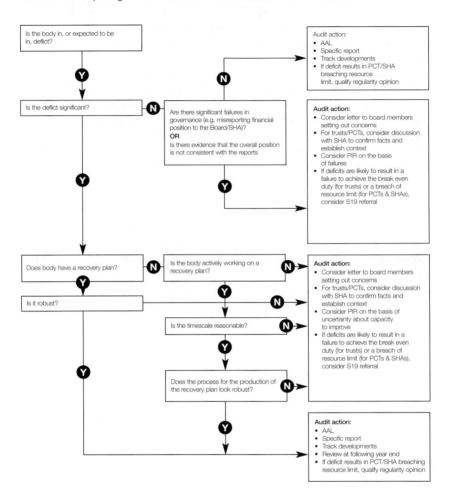

2 Chapter Two

Why Financial Recovery Plans May be Needed

Although organisations should always plan to manage activities within available resources, problems will inevitably arise. These can range from long standing underlying financial problems to one off occurrences where expected funding does not materialise.

Understanding that your organisation has a problem and identifying its root cause is a critical first step towards dealing with it. This is even more important under resource accounting and budgeting, which requires NHS organisations to recover deficits incurred in previous years.

It is important to bear in mind that financial problems are likely to be linked to, or caused by, service and/or organisational difficulties. When identifying the underlying root causes it is therefore essential that financial issues are not viewed in isolation: organisational and service challenges must also be considered if long term sustainability is to be achieved.

The remainder of this chapter looks at circumstances that have led to the need for recovery plans and are therefore things to watch out for in your own organisation. All examples are taken from real life situations.

Structural imbalance

A health economy may be out of balance in structural terms. For example, an area may have too many relatively small hospitals serving small catchment populations. This creates a problem in relation to sustaining critical mass and leads to operational inflexibility and consequential increased costs. This can be further compounded by the existence of a large number of community hospitals. The overall infrastructure may not be affordable or sustainable within the current and future level of funding.

There may also be structural or configuration problems within an organisation - for example, if a trust operates across a number of different sites there may be a lack of consistency in managerial, governance or clinical systems and practice. There may also be difficulties arising from poor integration between the various sites.

Funding

Funding may be expected but not received. For example, the initial cost of a non-recurrent project at a trust may be funded by the Department of Health with the trust assuming that PCTs will fund future related recurrent costs. If those monies are not forthcoming, the trust faces a funding gap.

The implementation of payment by results (PbR) will have a significant impact on the money received by trusts from PCTs.

Demand and 'over-trading'

The rate at which a population accesses services may exceed expectations and therefore cause problems as funding levels cannot keep pace. This can lead to 'over-trading' with PCTs either funding higher levels of activity than are affordable or NHS trusts treating more patients than they are being funded for. This creates a major financial pressure within local health and social care communities. This 'excess met demand' may be exacerbated further as PbR is introduced and poses a significant challenge to PCT commissioners who have to manage demand.

Supply and 'under-trading'

Over supply or lower than expected demand for services can also cause significant problems, particularly as a large proportion of the associated costs is likely to be fixed. This 'excess supply' will also be exacerbated further as PbR comes on stream.

High costs

Although the weighted capitation formula used to allocate resources to PCTs is adjusted for the market forces factor and high labour costs, these may not adequately compensate for the additional costs of providing healthcare in some areas. The overall cost of living is also high in some areas and this increases the non-pay costs of service providers.

Staffing costs

Some areas have trouble attracting staff - for example, the cost of housing and the competitive salaries offered in the South East are major obstacles to attracting and retaining staff in the NHS. Most trusts in this area are therefore heavily dependent on agency, bank and locum staff. This adds considerably to employment costs. Staff shortages also have implications for the overall capacity of an area to deliver healthcare.

Delayed transfers of care

In some areas delayed transfer of care can cause particular problems with large numbers of beds blocked by patients who no longer need to be in an acute environment. This has a serious impact on operational efficiency and leads to significant financial pressures. This problem may be particularly acute in areas where local authorities face financial challenges.

Low productivity

Low levels of productivity can lead to problems. Sometimes this can be caused - at least in part - by a lack of critical mass but it can also be attributed to a tendency to create new unaffordable capacity in response to the need to meet NHS Plan targets rather than utilising existing capacity and facilities more effectively.

Weak financial management

In some areas inadequate financial discipline and control may result in poor financial planning and decision-making leading to, for example:

- Unaffordable commitments
- Poor capital planning and business cases
- Investment decisions that have exacerbated the underlying financial problem
- Weak systems of internal financial control and accountability
- A deficit culture and expectation that organisations will be 'bailed out' if they overspend.

Flexibility

Some organisations may have trouble adapting to the lack of financial flexibility now available. For example, there is no longer an ability to vire funds from capital to revenue.

Focus on short-term 'fixes' rather than systemic change

In some areas there is a history of year-end 'fixes' - managing the year-end on a 'fire-fighting' basis using short-term measures and non-recurrent solutions rather than thinking of longer-term recovery and stability.

Organisational change

Accelerating change is now a way of life for all organisations and unless there is a proactive approach to financial planning, instability, financial turbulence and low morale can be caused.

Lack of leadership

Instability in the senior management structure and/ or no clear direction can lead to a lack of focus, poor decision making and frequent unsettling changes of approach. At an organisational level, a lack of clarity between PCTs and trusts about lead commissioning can result in problems in agreeing service level agreements.

Failure to deliver

In some areas, earlier 'performance improvement plans' and FRPs have not been delivered - this means that 'old' problems and difficulties still need to be addressed. Sometimes this is because the root causes of the deficit have not been identified. Financial problems invariably reflect operational failings within an organisation and these need to be looked into. There may also be difficulties in terms of management capacity or capability - any skills shortages need to identified and dealt with.

3 Chapter Three

How to Develop a Financial Recovery Plan

As mentioned in chapter 1, there is no single 'right' approach to drawing up a FRP. However, from looking at a number of NHS examples there appear to be a series of steps that are common - each is discussed in the chapters that follow:

- Understanding where the organisation is now and why: look at the baseline position; diagnose the nature and scale of the problem and identify the root causes and contributory factors. Look at financial, organisational and service issues. Accept that there is a problem that needs to be addressed (see chapter 4)

- Make sure there is corporate ownership and a recognition that it is not just a finance problem; involve all those affected, including clinicians, others that are key to delivering improved productivity and cost efficiencies and organisations within the wider health economy; make sure you have sustained commitment from them; establish clear accountabilities - who is going to do what and when? Make sure that overall aims and direction are clear (see chapter 5)

- Look at the context: what is the FRP aiming to achieve and how does that sit with overall organisational objectives? What impact does the national policy agenda have - for example modernisation and the introduction of patient choice and payment by results? What about any wider healthcare economy aims - remember that the FRP should be an integral part of local health community plans. Think of both the short and long term (see chapter 6)

- Identify productivity and cost improvement measures: how and where can things be done more effectively and efficiently? Where can costs be reduced or avoided? Use tools such as benchmarking and the Department of Health's 'high impact changes' to help focus on the most promising options; think about short term 'quick wins' as well as medium to longer term solutions; think about risks that could prevent the achievement of plans and prepare contingency arrangements (see chapter 7)

- Formalise the FRP - make sure it is practical and realistic; secure agreement and confirm accountabilities; ensure that there is a process for monitoring the FRP's implementation and for reviewing the FRP process itself: identify any learning/ improvement points (see chapter 8).

At a more detailed level it may also be helpful to bear in mind the points emphasised by the Audit Commission at recent HFMA seminars. Namely that FRPs must be robust and should:

- Be based on prudent/ realistic assumptions
- Address the reasons that cause the overspend
- Aim to achieve recurrent balance by the end of the period (3/5 years)
- Aim to recover historic deficits
- Differentiate between recurrent and non-recurrent expenditure
- Be translated into action plans with responsibilities and timescales
- Be fully integrated into operational plans (for example, LDPs/ NHS Plan targets)
- Be understood and supported by the board, managers and clinicians
- Be developed with and supported by all bodies in the health economy
- Be updated regularly to take account of changed circumstances.

As well as looking at the practical examples set out in the chapters that follow, health bodies may be able to gain insights from the experiences of other sectors. For example, research carried out by the Office of the Deputy Prime Minister (ODPM) into local authority practice has identified a number of key characteristics for a good recovery plan[3]:

- Honesty - there needs to be realism when assessing the current situation, the challenges faced, the capacity to respond and the time and resources it will take to deliver
- Brevity - the plan needs to be concise and focussed and although details of who needs to do what and when are needed in operational terms they need not necessarily appear in the main document
- Prioritisation - so that attention is focussed on key areas
- Accountability - so that responsibilities for delivery are clear.

---

[3] Local authority recovery plans tend to be wider in scope (ie they go beyond financial recovery) and are linked to the 'comprehensive performance assessment' regime.

The ODPM has also identified 9 key elements that are common to good recovery plans:

- Capacity - an assessment of whether or not the capacity/ resources (finance, personnel and skills) exist to deliver the planned improvements
- Support - whether support is needed to deliver the plan and the nature of that support (short/ long term; in-house/ external)
- Programme and project management arrangements - how the plan will be managed, co-ordinated and evaluated
- Timescales - for achieving priorities along with milestones and measurable outcomes. This may include short, medium and long term timeframes
- Performance measures/ indicators - measures for success relating to each priority
- Targets - challenging but achievable, designed to encourage and monitor progress
- Monitoring - arrangements to monitor progress
- Risks - an assessment of risks (internal/ external) relating to delivery of the plan and mitigation strategies/contingency plans
- Links - to other plans and processes so that other areas are not adversely affected.

If you want to know more about best practice in local authorities visit the local government pages of the ODPM's website and type in 'recovery plans' to the search box:

http://www.odpm.gov.uk/stellent/groups/odpm_localgov/documents/sec tionhomepage/odpm_localgov_page.hcsp

Chapter Four

Establishing the Baseline Position

An organisation needs to know where it stands so that it can plan its recovery. The first stage in developing a FRP involves looking at the current financial position and understanding why you are where you are. This needs to include a review not only of the financial state of play but also the underlying organisational and service issues.

In particular, organisations need to identify the problems faced and their causes and understand why the financial position is as it is. From a narrower financial perspective, you need to think about whether difficulties relate to recurrent or non-recurrent elements. It is also important to assess likely current and future trends and review the overall approach - for example:

- Why are you where you are? (See chapter 2)
- Do your difficulties arise from recurrent or non-recurrent elements?
- Has the problem stabilised or is it expected to worsen?
- What will be the impact of new policy developments - for example, patient choice and payment by results?
- How will your organisation's strategies and objectives affect the position?
- What are your predictions in terms of financial outturn?
- Can you meet your cash requirements?
- Are your financial control systems robust?
- Are your financial management procedures 'fit for purpose'?
- Where do you want to get to?

This assessment needs to be handled carefully otherwise there is a danger that it becomes a means of apportioning blame. To avoid this, make sure that all those affected understand that the ultimate purpose is to identify ways of doing things better and to improve personal and organisational performance for the benefit of patients.

Establishing an organisation's financial outturn is clearly important at this stage. As part of this process it is helpful to explain how the financial gap has arisen and include realistic assessments (magnitude and likelihood) of any associated risks. For example for 2004/05 these could include:

- SLA volume risks
- The impact of agenda for change
- The level of early retirements.

It is also important to assess and understand strengths and weaknesses within the local health community and how they may help or hinder the development and implementation of FRPs. For example, there may be a need to change attitudes before progress is possible.

5 Chapter Five

Ownership and Communication

FRPs are not the sole responsibility of finance departments and it is important that the underlying problem and the proposed way forward are 'owned' and understood from the outset (ie prior to implementation) by the whole organisation and its partners. FRPs need sustained commitment from all those affected if they are to succeed. This means that an organisation needs to think about communication processes early on and ensure that everyone who needs to be involved is aware of the situation. Accountabilities must also be clear from the start.

One PCT's approach to ensuring that there is corporate 'buy in' is based on a recognition that key stakeholders have different roles to play. This is summarised below:

Leadership[4] through:

• Chief executive
• Chair and non executive directors
• Chair of the professional executive committee (PEC)

Ownership[5] through:

• Executive directors
• Senior managers
• Budget holders

Awareness through:

• Whole organisation

---

[4] It is important that the leadership team itself commits to the process: developing a FRP is not a part time job. The process leaders must also have the necessary project management, influencing and communication skills.

[5] Clinicians will generate a high proportion of recurrent savings - they must therefore be 'on board' from the outset.

Early communication:

- To partners (a 2 way process).

The recognition that developing a FRP affects the entire organisation and the wider health economy is further emphasised in this PCT by 'sharing the pain' and making responsibilities clear:

- Allocate targets to each director (including the clinical side)
- Draft ideas tested at senior management team
- Directors to work with teams and partner organisations for sign up and ownership
- Discussed and approved by PEC and board
- SHA, overview and scrutiny committee and public engagement
- Progress monitored through: performance management framework; board assurance framework; relevant internal groups; accountability agreement
- Personal commitment by chief executive.

Hinchingbrooke Health Care NHS Trust's Financial Improvement Plan (FIP) recognises that without a clear communications strategy, the plan's objectives may not be achieved.

In particular the FIP identifies aims for communicating effectively about the plan as being to:

- Explain how the trust's finance works in understandable terms
- Explain how budgets are calculated
- Emphasise the importance of budget holders spending within their budgets
- Make all staff aware of the financial consequences of their actions
- Put finance at the top of everyone's agenda to provide the highest possible standards of patient care.

Hinchingbrooke has also used a 'branded campaign' to ensure that staff understand the reasons for and objectives of the FIP. This includes launching the FIP to clinicians, senior managers and staff with opportunities for discussion; road shows throughout the hospital; finance notice boards at strategic points with progress reports and information; budget surgeries to give advice to budget holders; rewards for good ideas about how money could be spent better; identifying 'champions for financial success'.

At this stage it is also worth thinking in broad terms about the approach an organisation intends to follow and whether or not there is scope for a number of parallel development strands. For example, Secta group ltd suggests that after diagnosing the problem a multi track FRP strategy could be considered focussing on 3 aspects:

- Immediate expenditure constraints - for example, quick cash releasing efficiency savings (CRES) wins and cost control
- Cost improvement programme - for example over the next 12 months and in relation to the 1/2-year CRES target. Also non-recurrent initiatives and service re-design
- Cost avoidance plans - for example, access/ capacity investment plans; prescribing expenditure growth; demand management.

An organisation also needs to think - again in broad terms - about the timetable for developing and implementing the FRP. For example it may decide to identify a series of key events or milestones and how these should be communicated - those set out by Surrey and Sussex SHA are shown below:

Milestones to delivering the financial recovery programme

The programme should be developed in line with best project management practice. The following list of key events is broadly ordinal. The actual amount of time taken will depend upon circumstances.

Key events:
1. The case for the initiation of a financial recovery programme is

presented to the board together with an initial cost estimate of completing the first logical part of the programme

2. The board approves the case to initiate a financial recovery programme and establish a board committee to oversee the preparation of the FRP for the consideration of the board within 3 months
3. The committee appoints a programme director
4. The programme director sets the organisation structure required.

The organisational structure of the recovery programme and the membership of key groups will depend on the key changes that need to be designed and the culture and capacity of the people who are to deliver the change. The organisation may include the following:

- Focus groups to prepare and implement the plan. Each focus group to be chaired by a member of the board committee and be accountable to the board committee.
- Technical support group to appraise the strategic fit, affordability, feasibility of implementation and value for money (costs - benefits - risks) of each option recommended by the focus groups. Membership of the technical support group will be situational, however is likely to include, senior financial analyst, internal auditor (finance), information analyst, head of clinical audit, human resources specialist and relevant clinical specialists.
- A liaison officer to liaise with other agencies to negotiate agreement to progress schemes that require approval from other agencies.

5. The plan is presented to the board and upon its approval accountability for its delivery will be assigned to trust executives. The focus groups may be retained to support the delivery of the plan
6. At each meeting of the board accountable executive will report progress in their delivery of agreed plans.

At the same time it is important that organisations do not view their approach to developing a FRP as being 'set in stone': if 'quick wins' are identified they should be pursued.

Aims and Context

FRPs cannot be developed in a vacuum: their aims must be consistent with an organisation's overall objectives and those of the wider healthcare community. They also need to take account of new national policy developments such as payment by results. If these different influences are not recognised and taken account of, there is a risk that actions taken to recover the financial position could lead to problems elsewhere.

It is also important to recognise that the first objective in any recovery process is likely to involve stabilising the situation and ensuring that financial controls are in place and effective. There is no point developing a comprehensive plan for future financial health if an organisation has not got the basics right first.

The importance of making sure that underlying systems and processes are 'fit for purpose' is reflected in the approach adopted in Surrey and Sussex. Here the SHA has developed a broad recovery strategy designed to help NHS organisations within its area 'overcome their underlying financial deficits and or financial risks and to deliver the NHS plan within financially sustainable balanced local health economies.' The underlying principle of this guidance is that 'delivering financial health and best clinical practice are inextricably linked and jointly prerequisite to demonstrating good value for patients.' In other words without a good underlying financial strategy you cannot deliver good healthcare and vice versa.

Establishing 'good habits' in relation to financial information and processes can also result in tangible benefits. For example, one PCT constantly reviews its reserves and balance sheet to identify:

- Any unusual creditors that may be reversible
- Cash flexibilities
- Any gains in interest on working balances
- Any temporary or permanent gains that can be made from items reserved at the start of the year
- Any provisions that can be reversed - for example in relation to 'old' premature retirements.

It is also important to factor in the impact of ever growing government and public expectations. One PCT has recognised that this means:

- Working with local trusts and neighbouring PCTs to modernise or re-engineer the system so that it can be sustained in the long term
- Looking at alternative service delivery models - for example, chronic disease management is crucial if pressure is to be taken off acute trusts
- Looking at ways of improving self care by patients - for example, the expert patient programme
- Adopting a whole system view of the care pathway.

In terms of the overall financial strategy for NHS organisations in Surrey and Sussex, 6 strategic aims have been identified which focus very much on the need to establish sound financial control and governance foundations. The 6 aims are shown below:

1. Improving Financial Health

- Strengthen financial management processes and systems of internal control
- Develop the capacity and capability of the finance function to ensure that it is 'fit for purpose'
- Implement FRPs to achieve underlying financial balance
- Acquire strategic/transitional financial support to enable and facilitate financial recovery and service reconfiguration.

2. Optimise Capital Investment

- Invest capital in schemes that optimise financial recovery and the delivery of the NHS Plan locally.

3. Effective Cash Management

- Improve internal cash management processes
- Manage the risk of cash shortfall.

4. Optimise the NHS Estate

- Ensure that the NHS estate is used effectively
- Sell sites that are surplus to requirement to avoid the unnecessary capital costs of holding estate that is surplus to requirements
- Generate capital receipts to contribute to cash management strategy
- Address backlog maintenance to optimise the balance between maintenance costs and replace / refurbishment.

5. Productivity/Efficiency - back office functions

- Review the scope and opportunity for shared service arrangements and outsourcing
- Modernise procurement practices and processes to deliver more effective purchasing arrangements and significant non-pay savings.

6. Financial Flows/Payments by Results

- Improve the efficiency and effectiveness of health service commissioning
- Implement plans to introduce Payments by Results
- Assess and manage the risks to individual organisations.

For each of these broad aims, the SHA set out delivery targets for the next 3 years, with detailed (quarter by quarter) actions for 2004/05. Risks to delivery, strengths, 'SHA enabling strategies' and Trusts' delivery plans have also been identified - see Appendix 1.

Hinchingbrooke Health Care NHS Trust also sets clear objectives for its Financial Improvement Plan (FIP) but the approach is different. Here the overall objective of the FIP is:

'To strengthen financial performance across the trust so that:

- The short term financial management performance will achieve the Trust's required targets in 2004/05 and 2005/06
- The financial health of the organisation is improved to ensure the

use of existing resources and new investment support the improvement of services for patients
- A better understanding of the Trust's financial position is promoted across the organisation so that the current cultural approach to finance can be changed.'

To achieve these overarching aims, the Trust has identified seven different 'elements' that need to be looked at:

- Expenditure (workforce, sourcing/ procurement, productivity, medicines management, process and cost controls)
- Income (commissioner income, choice, private patients, non patient income)
- Technical issues (financial flows, reference costs, budget flexing, resource allocation, budget re-basing)
- Finance team infrastructure (people, systems, information, training)
- Culture (board, clinicians, managers, staff)
- Performance management (performance management framework, benchmarking, incentives, training and development)
- External support (from external stakeholders such as audit, commissioners, SHA).

The FIP then identifies objectives, action plans and measurable outcomes for each.

Hinchingbrooke's FIP recognises that each element contributes in different ways to the trust's overall aims and that not all action plans are designed to generate measurable outputs in financial terms. Instead the FIP is seeking to ensure that the FIP process results in both cost improvements and a change in the underlying culture.

Another approach is to think in terms of strategic themes that can generate savings and result in long term stability.

For example, in Hampshire and the Isle of Wight, six areas have been identified under an overall banner of 'fixing the money':

- Continuing care

- Chronic disease management
- Unscheduled care
- Medicines management
- Diagnostics
- Back office functions/ Gershon review.

7 Cost Improvement

Once an organisation has made sure that its approach to financial control and management is robust, it needs to think of ways of delivering financial recovery. This means looking for cost savings, both in the short and longer term - it is important to ensure that there is sufficient capacity to deliver both.

Quick wins

It is worth looking first at easy and quick wins - 'low hanging fruit'. For example, an organisation could save thousands each year by switching to second-class post or using lighter weight (and cheaper) paper. Reducing non-clinical room temperatures by 1 degree centigrade saved £20,000 in one acute trust. Some trusts have also used 'reverse auctioning' for drugs and stationery procurement.

Organisations should also look into the possibility of introducing tax efficient employment contracts using a salary sacrifice scheme - for example the home computing initiative or work place nurseries/childcare vouchers.

In one acute trust a number of quick wins were identified by controlling and managing purchasing. As well as establishing a collaborative approach to procurement and strategic supplier relationships, the trust identified the following savings through price improvement and product standardisation:

- Contrast media standardised and volume discount (£75,000)
- Radiology film standardised and volume discount (£60,000)
- Orthopaedic casting standardised (£7,000)

In PCTs a key pressure is GP prescribing. One PCT's approach has aimed to achieve:

- Improved generic prescribing rate
- Reduced inappropriate prescribing
- Better linkage between primary and secondary care (price duality

issues and discharge processes)
- Improved awareness of prescribing trends amongst GPs
- Improved linkage between quality prescribing agenda and resource management
- Pharmacists working directly with GPs.

In Hampshire and the Isle of Wight SHA, primary and secondary care use joint formularies and dressings to reduce wastage.

It is important to bear in mind that some easy to identify savings will be non recurrent and so will have only a short-term impact.

Medium to longer-term savings

Material cost improvements can range from relatively straightforward improvements to services and productivity to large-scale system re-designs, service reconfiguration or site rationalisations.

One systematic way of looking at savings is to follow the approach adopted by Hampshire and Isle of Wight SHA, which requires FRPs to distinguish between three 'savings levels':

- Level 1 - organisational CRES (trusts and PCTs). These are cash releasing and efficiency savings being made by the organisation. Examples are: income generation, savings on non-pay (cost and volume) and savings on pay (i.e. skill mix changes)
- Level 2 - organisational modernisation (trusts and PCTs). These are savings made internally to the organisation through service redesign and improvements that create efficiencies
- Level 3 - health economy wide transformation and improvement. These are savings that are inter-dependent on other organisations. They will relate to the strategic programme, together with other locality led savings schemes. Examples are: joint management structures, demand management, strategic service change across the locality (i.e. shared pathology).

Atos Consulting Ltd suggest 4 approaches to performance improvement:

- Benchmarking and diagnostics - Atos Consulting suggest functional benchmarking against an appropriate peer group to identify individual departments where performance improvement can be pursued. For example, in one trust, functional benchmarking indicated that neurology varied significantly in terms of gross cost and unit cost from the peer group. Specifically, the benchmarking data showed that pay per consultant was higher than the peer group, follow up to new ratios in outpatients were higher than the peer group and subsequently that new attendances were lower than the peer group. Following a closer analysis of activity data by consultant and discussion with key managers the two key actions taken were to replace 2 long-term locums with substantive posts, and to work with one particular consultant to reduce his number of follow up appointments by developing care protocols which could be adopted by the primary care sector
- Priority based service review (PBSR) - here the emphasis is on understanding how the current level of service provided within a department compares to a mandatory level of service and to an enhanced model. Using this model it is possible to define the service and financial impact of changing the level of service to the enhanced model, the mandatory model or a model somewhere in-between. By way of an example, it was acknowledged that the implementation of recommendations made within the Audit Commission report 'A spoonful of sugar' offered an opportunity to enhance service whilst reducing cost where the recommendations were correctly implemented
- Supply chain transformation - this approach focuses on reducing non-pay spend across the organisation. At its simplest level supply chain transformation reduces non-pay spend through areas such as controlling demand, adopting and adhering to policies, product standardisation, supplier rationalisation and price. At a more strategic level, opportunities exist around strategic sourcing and logistics. Although supply chain transformation focuses on non-pay, it is important to understand how pay and service can be impacted. To expand on the 'spoonful of sugar' example, if a constraint to achieving ward based technicians is the ability to recruit, robotics

could be introduced which release dispensary technicians to adopt ward based roles

- Clinical modelling - here the focus is on patient flows and releasing key blockages in the system. For example, in one trust it was found that 25% of A&E admissions were avoidable and inappropriate. To address this problem, admission protocols were redefined and the role of A&E consultants re-focussed. A key piece of work around admissions supported by enhanced numbers of ward rounds have been key drivers behind one Trust being able to close over 100 beds in the one year.

Benchmarking

Whatever cost improvement measures your organisation is considering an early step should be to benchmark your own approach and results against others. Any significant variations in clinical or financial performance are an indication that more detailed comparisons would be worthwhile as it is in these areas where savings are most likely to be found. In particular it is a good idea to look at and compare:

- Inputs and outputs - for example, compare spending levels in key areas such as fuel and energy, agency staff and prescribing (primary and acute settings)
- Peer comparison and variation - for example, undertake a benchmark comparison of your staff turnover and absenteeism rates
- Department specific factors - for example, patient admission processes
- Cost driver specific factors - for example, lengths of stay and prescribing.

Useful sources for benchmarking information include:

- The Healthcare Commission's acute hospitals portfolio (delivered by the Audit Commission)
- The Department of Health's reference costs - how far is your organisation from the standardised reference cost index?
- The CIPFA database - this covers trust and PCT TACs and TFRs
- Functional cost benchmarking - looking at where money is spent and what the unit costs are. Where spend and unit costs are relatively high

there may be scope for improvement. Where spend and unit costs are low there may be quality and risk issues

- Clinical productivity and outcomes
- Local and professional information.

Surrey and Sussex SHA identified the following indicators as being useful when looking for opportunities to deliver financial recovery:

1. Benchmark comparison of spending in key areas, such as
   - Fuel and energy
   - Agency
   - Prescribing (primary and acute settings)
2. Benchmark comparison of human resource management, such as
   - Staff turnover rate
   - Absenteeism rate
3. Distance from standardised reference cost index
4. Number of beds blocked by delayed transfers of care
5. Day case % statistics
6. Length of stay for non-day case
7. Utilisation rates of beds and operating theatres by specialty
8. Number of infections
9. Cancellation of operations and operating sessions statistics.

Hampshire and the Isle of Wight SHA has developed a benchmarking model for trusts and PCTs that also looks at a range of indicators:

Acute trusts

Financial performance
- Cost of drugs/ specialty cost for general medicine, general surgery, rheumatology and dermatology as calculated in the reference cost exercise (%s)
- High level reference cost indicators based on top 10 indices by volume (£s)

Workforce performance (all %s)
- Agency costs/ staffing group pay costs for medical staffing, nursing and other

- Bank costs/ staffing group pay costs for medical staffing, nursing and other
- Management cost/ turnover
- Sickness and absence/ actual available hours

Service efficiency
- ALOS by HRGs for top 10 (in days)
- Day case rates by specialty for general surgery, urology, orthopaedics, ENT, ophthalmology, maxillofacial, general medicine, paediatrics, gynaecology, haematology (ie the % of FCEs dealt with as day cases)
- Number of delayed discharges/ total admissions (%)
- Theatre downtime/ theatre availability (assume 24/7 availability) as a %

Access (as %s)
- Number of cancelled operations/ total FFCEs
- RTAs/ A&E attendances.

PCTs

Financial performance
- Prescribing costs/ total revenue resource limit (RRL) as a %
- Net ingredient cost/ ASTRO PU (divided by 1000) in £s
- Continuing care costs (excluding s28a and special placements)/ total RRL (%)
- Cost of s28a agreements for continuing care/ total RRL (%)
- Special placements costs/ total RRL (%)
- Cost of old long stay / total RRL (%)

Workforce performance (all %s)
- Agency costs/ staffing group pay costs for medical staffing (elderly, community and LD), nursing (elderly, community and LD) and other (elderly, community and LD)
- Bank costs/ staffing group pay costs for medical staffing (elderly, community and LD), nursing (elderly, community and LD) and other (elderly, community and LD)
- Management costs/ net turnover (ie after removing commissioning related turnover)

- Sickness and absence/ actual available hours

Service efficiency
- GP referrals to secondary care (by specialty)/ weighted population (%).

Action plans

Once benchmarking has been used to identify the most promising areas for finding cost improvements organisations need to come up with specific measures or schemes that will generate those savings and draw up action plans for their achievement. Issues that should be thought about when looking at a particular proposal include:

- The impact on services - will it affect the delivery of agreed service performance? What impact will the change have in human and organisational terms? Are there any reconfiguration issues?
- The capacity of the organisation itself - does your organisation have the people and or skills necessary to implement the proposal? Does it need to think about filling any capability gaps?
- Risks - 'what if scenarios': What could upset your organisation's plans and what would the impact be? Are there any barriers to change? What will be the effects of payment by results?
- How well does the proposal fit with other strategies and plans?
- What level of savings does your organisation expect to generate and in what timescale? How 'comfortable' are these targets? How likely is it that they will be achieved?
- What other benefits could the proposal lead to and over what timescale? What does your organisation need to do to make sure they are realised?
- Who is going to do what and when?
- How is your organisation going to make sure everyone knows and understands the planned route? For example, share outline action plans with those affected and get their commitment: communicate and consult.

It makes sense to involve a wide range of people from different backgrounds and with different interests and skills when identifying cost improvement proposals. This way your organisation should come up with a long list of potential schemes that can be sifted. For each scheme that is selected management responsibility for its delivery should be identified.

In Hampshire and Isle of Wight SHA, each savings scheme that is included in a FRP must be accompanied by 'sufficient detail to enable the scheme to be taken forward and implemented'. In practice this means that the detailed programmes should:

- Provide an explanation of the specific schemes
- Identify a 'lead manager' who is responsible for implementing and monitoring each scheme
- Include completion dates for each scheme
- Include details on the monitoring and implementation process to ensure the delivery of schemes
- Where there are schemes yet to be identified for the remaining balance, describe the processes that are underway to address this on a non-recurrent basis (for example, freezing vacancies)
- Include a risk assessment and countermeasures for non-achievement.

Register of FRP schemes

To help organisations in its area, the Surrey and Sussex SHA maintains and updates regularly a 'register of financial recovery schemes'.
The December 2004 version is attached as appendix 3.

Modernisation Agency

Another useful source of ideas is the Modernisation Agency's 'Ten Ways to Shake the World'. Issued as an HSJ supplement on 9 September 2004, this booklet identifies the following 10 'high impact changes that can transform a trust's performance':

- Treat day surgery as the norm for elective surgery
- Improve patient flows across the NHS system by improving access to diagnostic tests
- Manage variation in patient discharge to reduce length of stay

- Manage variation in patient admissions
- Avoid unnecessary follow-ups for patients
- Increase the reliability of therapeutic interventions through a 'care bundle' approach
- Apply a systematic approach to care for people with long term conditions
- Improve patient access by reducing the number of queues
- Optimise patient flow through service bottlenecks using process templates
- Redesign and extend staff roles in line with efficient patient pathways to attract and retain an effective workforce.

The booklet includes case studies and guidance on 'what to do next' and is available from www.modern.nhs.uk/highimpactchanges. This site also contains a guide for PCTs which sets out how they can use the 10 changes 'to:

- Underpin their local improvement strategy
- Improve the services they provide
- Negotiate a better deal for patients from the services they commission and the organisations they contract with.'

Risk assessment

Before action plans for your cost improvement measures can be finalised you need to think through risk issues. Every FRP should include a realistic assessment of the risks associated with the delivery of each key component or proposal. As with any risk assessment it is important to think through the impact, probability, sensitivity and materiality. Contingency measures should also be set out in case any of the risks actually happen

A PCT identified the overall risks to achieving its FRP as being:

- Capacity to deliver
- Inadequate planning
- Shortened timescales
- Over optimistic estimate of savings
- Resistance in partner organisations - councillors for political reasons

and clinicians because of an unwillingness to change
- Priorities of partner organisations
- GPs - independent contractors
- Reduced investment in key areas and other in year cost pressures
- Public involvement.

Hinchingbrooke Health Care NHS Trust's FIP requires those with responsibility for delivering each item in the action plans to keep an up to date log of risks using a standard format. This requires details of:

- The element the risk relates to
- Details of the risk itself
- The odds of the risk arising
- The potential impact of the risk
- A description of the impact
- Risk management activity.

The risks are assessed by Hinchingbrooke's steering group, which makes recommendations about mitigation strategies.

Another NHS trust classifies its risks across three headings:

- Clinical and service - for example, workforce or technology requirements change
- Financial - for example, the PbR implementation timetable alters
- Operational - for example, workforce needs cannot be met.

Risks to delivery in Surrey and Sussex SHA are included in Appendix 1.

Formalise, Monitor and Review

Once the FRP is finalised, sound arrangements need to be in place to make sure that its delivery is managed and progress monitored and controlled. To be effective, this means that there should be dedicated resources (a team, group or 'board') charged with specific responsibility for the FRP.

It is also important to think through the process for delivering the FRP so that an organisation can learn from any difficulties and do it better next time round. For example, it may be a good idea to review FRPs within a healthcare community to make sure assumptions are consistent and to eliminate any double counting between commissioners or providers. A review of your approach may also lead to timing changes - for example, in Hampshire and the Isle of Wight SHA, organisations have been encouraged to develop FRPs alongside the process of agreeing local delivery plans (LDPs) and service level agreements (SLAs) to minimise the possibility of slippage on schemes.

In Hinchingbrooke Health Care NHS Trust the Financial Improvement Plan is monitored by a steering group chaired by the chief executive and with membership including:

- Director of finance, information and performance
- Director of nursing, midwifery and operations
- Director of service improvement
- Medical director
- Director of human resources and communications
- Director of facilities
- Trust staff council chairman
- Medical advisory committee chairman
- Hunts PCT representative.

The steering group meets monthly and its role is to:

- Monitor the plan's progress in relation to actions/ outputs against timescales and benefits realisation
- Discuss risks to the delivery of FIP elements
- Recommend further actions to leads where progress is not in line

with the timescale
- Agree communications through the organisation about progress
- Report progress and risks to the board on a regular basis.

Example template FRPs as used in Surrey and Sussex and Hampshire and the Isle of Wight SHAs are reproduced at Appendix 2.

Tips for a Successful Financial Recovery Plan

Looking at a number of NHS examples and the comments made by speakers at the HFMA's seminars there are a number of issues that organisations need to get right if their FRPs are to be effective and meaningful. In broad terms these can be grouped as follows:

- Openness and honesty about the situation, within and outside the organisation
- Involvement and communication
- Managerial capacity and ability
- Sound financial, performance and risk management.

Openness and honesty

- Open and honest reporting
- Transparency - true scale of the problem laid bare for all to understand
- Express problem in service terms: get to the root cause, not the symptom
- Recognise that financial deficit is a symptom not a cause
- A clear well written and practical plan.

Involvement and communication

- Shared ownership and commitment across the health community
- Engage with clinicians where clinical re-design is proposed: get their active participation and commitment
- Communication, engagement and consultation throughout the FRP process
- Public involvement and acceptance.

Managerial capacity and ability

- Effective leadership
- Clear and effective management structure
- Clear responsibilities and accountabilities at all levels
- Strong operational and clinical management
- Adequate management capacity
- Be clear about the organisation's core business
- Monitor and plan for policy developments - for example, payment by results

- Be ruthless about low priority areas.

Sound financial, performance and risk management

- Early planning
- Stabilise the situation and get control before you move on: 'put the plug in the bath'
- Strong internal performance management
- Effective financial management
- Sound systems and processes
- Balance service and financial priorities
- Challenge current practice
- Embrace benchmarking
- Structural change - big problems require big solutions
- Identify risks and manage them
- More effective use of joint resources.

One trust identified 3 steps to success in FRP development as being:

- Clear purpose
- Clear leadership
- Collective and relentless pursuit of purpose.

Secta plc highlighted the following key critical success factors:

- Acting on the diagnosis phase: 'stop digging the hole'
- FRP is a change management process
- Develop an appropriate range of FRP strategies - not just one dimensional track
- Challenging CRES programme
- Invest in implementation and change planning - building organisational capacity
- Make FRP an integral part of your organisation's performance management culture
- Focus on robust risk assessment - timing issues and deliverability.

Surrey and Sussex SHA: preconditions for effective financial recovery

- Acceptance of the need for a FRP
- Delegated authority to implement financial recovery schemes that impact services
- Leadership focussed on the FRP including a programme director accountable to the board
- Capacity sufficient to support the programme director
- A clear deliverable plan
- Support for the implementation of the plan by the individuals who will be implementing the changes arising from it.

Accepting the need for financial recovery

NHS organisations must accept the need for a financial recovery programme if any of the following conditions exist:

- Current year to date or forecast deviation from full statutory compliance with financial duties
- Reported risks of an underlying financial problem exist after allowing for non-recurrent and full year effects of cost pressures and past initiatives to improve financial performance, and slippage in service developments
- Costs exceed standardised reference costs (national tariff)
- Current year to date or reported risk or forecast deviation from the key performance targets:

Delegated authority

Advice should be presented to the board of the need to initiate a FRP together with a recommended action plan to set up the essential financial recovery organisational framework.

Upon the decision of the board to initiate a FRP the trust board should set up a board committee and appoint a committee chairman from the board membership to prepare a FRP by a given date.

Authority should be delegated to the board committee to appoint a financial recovery programme director to draft and implement financial recovery schemes that impact services.

The board committee should have power to disband or direct existing groups set up within the trust to improve financial performance.
The committee may also set up focus groups and a technical support group to prepare and implement the plan.

Leadership

The board committee should exercise its' delegated authority to appoint a financial recovery programme director to draft and implement financial recovery schemes that impact services.

The financial recovery programme director should be accountable through the recovery committee to the board and personally present progress reports to the board.

Capacity

The board committee and the financial recovery programme director should be resourced so that it has adequate capacity to carry out its purpose.

The committee should ensure that it exercises this power and that it employs existing capacity in the form of existing groups set up within the trust to improve performance.

The board should approve the resources required when it agrees to initiate the financial recovery programme and appoint a programme director.

A clear plan

The FRP should clearly describe who is to do what when. The template FRP is provided in Appendix 2.

The FRP needs to demonstrate that the programme will be delivered within the pre-set timetable.

Support

The implementation of the plan must be agreed by the individuals who will be implementing the changes arising from it.

Possible pitfalls

Things to watch out for in relation to FRPs include:

- Plans are developed too late
- Plans do not address underlying financial problems
- Unidentified savings schemes are included
- There are 'gaps' in the plan
- The plan has not been agreed with stakeholders
- There is a history of not achieving targets
- There is a lack of ownership
- Over-reliance on non recurrent 'fixes'
- The plan is not seen as a 'live' document and not updated to take account of changed circumstances
- Progress against the plan is not monitored.

Appendix 1

Surrey and Sussex SHA Financial Strategy

In terms of the overall strategy for NHS organisations in Surrey and Sussex, six strategic aims have been identified which focus very much on the need to establish sound financial control and governance foundations. The remainder of this appendix looks at each aim in turn.

1. Improving Financial Health

Aims to

- Strengthen financial management processes and systems of internal control
- Develop the capacity of the finance function to ensure that it is 'fit for purpose'
- Implement financial recovery plans to restore underlying financial balance
- Acquire strategic/transitional financial support to enable and facilitate financial recovery and service reconfiguration.

Delivery Targets

2003/04

- Provided guidance to all NHS organisations in Surrey and Sussex on improving internal financial management systems and processes and strengthening financial discipline and control
- Provided a framework for financial recovery and described schemes, provided training and co-ordinated workshops
- Produced plans for improving systems of internal control
- Formalised finance staff development strategy and programme
- Established focus groups
- Set up financial planning matrix model integrating income and expenditure, investment and financial recovery plans.
- Delivered locally approved detail FRPs to underpin the LDPs of local health communities
- Ensured all organisations planned to comply with their statutory

financial duties
- Secured financial support (£40m 2003/04) from the NHS Bank to underpin and enable the process of service reconfiguration and financial recovery.

2004/05 as above plus:

- Focus on delivery of financial recovery targets
- Ensure local FRPs are effectively implemented and that the underlying recurrent financial deficit is significantly reduced
- Ensure all organisations achieve financial break-even in year
- Secure further financial support from the NHS Bank for the duration of the agreed financial recovery programme
- Provide direct leadership on strategic financial recovery schemes and support organisations through the process of financial recovery.

2005/06

- All local health communities, with the exception of those engaged in major service reconfiguration, to be back in underlying recurrent financial balance by April 2006
- Non-recurrent support to be identified and agreed for those local health communities engaged in major service reconfiguration to enable them to meet short-term financial targets.

2006/07

- Local health communities in Surrey and Sussex deliver the NHS Plan within a financially balanced health economy.

Risks to Delivery

- Continued failure of organisations to implement and deliver their FRPs
- Impact of new financial pressures and erosion of financial flexibility
- Managerial capacity and change overload
- Failure to secure adequate financial assistance from the NHS Bank
- Support from the NHS Bank having to be repaid in full or in part
- Weaknesses in controls assurance in financial management, governance and risk management.

Strengths

- SHA's financial planning processes (cited as an example of good practice by the Audit Commission)
- Availability of comprehensive guidance and a framework for financial recovery
- Experience of, and opportunity to learn from, past failures
- Good understanding of the underlying financial position and its causes.

SHA Enabling Strategies

- Capital investment strategy
- Training and development programme
- Performance management strategy
- Service improvement/modernisation strategy
- Productivity plan
- Demand management programme
- SHA led financial recovery schemes.

Trusts' Delivery Plans

- Source and application of funds statements supporting local delivery plans
- Financial recovery plans
- Investment plans
- Risk management and contingency plans.

Actions for 2004/05
(Note [R] denotes repeat each quarter)

Strategic Health Authority (SHA)

Quarter 1
- Issue SHA financial strategies and issue guidance (Done)
- Evaluate and advise on PCT and Trust FRPs and risk to delivery
- Confirm plans are robust or quantify risk
- Acquire financial support
- Set up controls assurance forum. Validate statements of internal control
- Deliver workshop - improving financial health
- Evaluate PCT/Trusts self-assessment of capacity and implementation

plans and advise accordingly
- Promote financial recovery through direct participation in meetings set up by Trusts and PCTs to deliver recovery and performance management. [R]

Quarter 2
- Validate performance reports against plans. Convene performance management meetings with PCTs and trusts. Report performance and present recommendations [R]
- Quantify financial risks.

Quarter 3
- Set financial planning framework for 2005/06
- Deliver workshop - financial planning - 2005/06.

Quarter 4
- Manage delivery of finance performance targets
- Complete financial plans for 2005/06.

PCTs and Trusts

Quarter 1
- Confirm local delivery plans, service level agreements, source and application of funds, investment and financial recovery plans, risk management strategies and contingency plans
- Deliver unqualified accounts for 2003/04 and statements of internal control
- Carry out self-assessment of capacity to deliver financial recovery and degree of corporate ownership
- In areas of high risk PCTs and trusts provide detailed implementation plans that demonstrate how improvement plans are to be delivered.

Quarter 2
- Present performance reports as required by SHA [R]
- Present plans to overcome control weaknesses declared in statements of internal control.

Quarter 4
Agree financial plans for 2005/06.

2. Optimise Capital Investment

Aims to

- Invest capital in schemes that optimise financial recovery and the delivery of the NHS Plan locally.

Delivery Targets

2003/04

- Established a capital investment team and agreed in principle a programme of strategic capital investment through to 2005/06 that enables service reconfiguration and transformation and supports financial recovery
- Established a capital investment database and financial reporting system.
- Commenced a programme of training and development in capital investment process and best practice for NHS organisations
- Reviewed schemes inherited from DHSC South and other schemes as presented
- Developed a high-level capital investment prioritisation methodology
- Managed strategic capital within the capital resource limit
- Progressed schemes key to the delivery of the transformation strategy.

2004/05 as above plus:

- Develop a detailed capital investment prioritisation methodology, carry out and evaluate a pilot study to inform the wider roll out of this across Surrey and Sussex
- Ensure that strategic outline cases are developed and approved where appropriate, and outline business cases are progressing into development for the major reconfiguration projects contained in the 'Transforming Health & Social Care Paper'
- Strategic service development plans are developed by PCTs to inform a primary care premises investment strategy
- Secure additional central capital to support the programme of service reconfiguration and transformation.

2005/06

- Outline business cases are approved and full business cases are in development for the major reconfiguration projects contained in the 'Transforming Health and Social Care Paper'
- Capital investment prioritisation criteria are rolled out across all NHS organisations - training and development to support implementation
- Primary care premises investment strategies are in place and a streamlined process for prioritisation and management of primary care premises investment is in place

Risks to Delivery

- The available capital funding is exceeded by the demands placed on it
- Central DH capital is constrained by badging against national priorities that reduce our ability to prioritise it locally
- Lack of sustainable revenue streams for supporting capital investment
- Payment by results, financial flows and patient choice regimes will put provider Trusts at risk, since PCTs will no longer have the ability to underwrite affordability on a long term basis
- The shortage of experienced manpower to manage capital investment projects in Surrey and Sussex
- Lack of Project Director expertise.

Key Strengths

- Strong capital investment knowledge base in the SHA
- Good linkages across SHA directorates to ensure prioritisation is well informed
- Good relationships between SHA capital investment team and DH leads
- Good communication network between SHA and PCT and Trust capital investment leads
- SHA has a strong capital investment reputation with DH
- SHA did not inherit an over-committed capital programme.

SHA Enabling Strategies

- 'Transforming Health and Social Care' in Surrey and Sussex, in particular to the process of major reconfiguration and modernisation
- Training and development programme

- Performance management strategy
- Optimise the NHS Estates - land receipts fund capital investment.

Trusts' Delivery Plans

- The activity assumptions of all NHS organisations' local delivery plans (LDPs) should be underpinned by capacity plans and local investment strategies and these should be in line with the financial assumptions in the source and application of funds that support the LDP.

Actions for 2004/05
Note [R] denotes repeat each quarter

Strategic Health Authority (SHA)

Quarter 1

- Draft detail prioritisation criteria
- Deliver workshop - improving capital investment
- Ensure that no schemes are approved that present a net cost pressure to local health communities with unspecified financial recovery plans and uncovered risks [R]
- Secure additional capital to fund Transformation Strategy.

Quarter 2

- Evaluate Estate Strategies and provide recommendation to PCTs and Trusts to optimise estate
- Validate capital investment plans against LDPs.
- Convene meetings with PCTs and Trusts. Report linkage between plans and progress against plans and present recommendations [R]
- Circulate capital investment strategy and guidance to PCTs and Trusts.

Quarter 3

- Deliver workshop - improving capital investment.

Quarter 4

- Evaluate capital investment plans for 2005/06.

PCTs and Trusts

Quarter 1
- Align capital investment plans to capacity requirements and LDPs.
- Update or confirm estates strategies.

Quarter 2
- Present performance reports as required by SHA [R]
- Comment on capital investment strategy and guidance.

Quarter 4
- Update capital investment plans for 2005/06.

3. Effective Cash Management

Aims to

- Improve internal cash management processes
- Manage the risk of cash shortfall.

Delivery Targets

2003/04
- Assessed cash brokerage requirements across Surrey and Sussex in accordance with the process established by the NHS Bank
- Established a strategy for managing cash within the resources available
- Ensured cash limits and EFLs were not exceeded by PCTs and NHS trusts
- Improved performance with respect to the PSPP target.

2004/05 as above plus:
- Improve the liquidity position of all organisations in Surrey and Sussex and reduce the requirement for external cash brokerage by at least 25% through balance sheet management and improved processes.

2005/06

- Use capital receipts from the disposal of surplus property to improve liquidity and restore working capital. Reduce the requirement for external cash brokerage by a further 25%.

2006/07

- Further improve liquidity and reduce the requirement for external cash brokerage by a further 25% by the generation of capital receipts.

2007/08

- Health economy to be self sufficient in terms of cash management with no requirement for external cash brokerage.

Risks to Delivery

- Failure of organisations to achieve break-even
- Failure of FRPs leading to increased cash requirements
- Weak internal processes for managing cash effectively
- Failure to deliver capital receipts to address underlying cash shortfall
- Reduced brokerage available through the NHS bank
- Failure of NHS Bank to resolve underlying cash imbalances.

Key Strengths

- Cash monitoring system in operation
- Cash management group meets quarterly
- Cash brokerage network confirmed
- The above systems delivered cash targets in 2003/04.

SHA Enabling Strategies

- Optimise NHS estate - generates cash.

Trusts' Delivery Plans

- Cash management timetable
- FRPs should include cash management.

Actions for 2004/05

Note [R] denotes repeat each quarter

Strategic Health Authority (SHA)

Quarter 1

- Cash management focus group review year end cash management identify opportunities for improvement
- Agree local plans for improving internal cash management processes and achieving improved liquidity
- Estimate underlying cash deficit
- Draft cash management strategy and issue draft guidance
- Validate PCT and trust plans and advise all concerned
- Request financial support.

Quarter 2

- Validate performance reports against cash flow forecasts
- Convene performance management meetings with PCTs and trusts
- Report performance and present recommendations. [R]

Quarter 3

- Deliver workshop - effective cash management.

Quarter 4

- Confirm availability of cash brokerage with NHS Bank
- Manage year-end cash positions across SHA.

PCTs and Trusts

Quarter 1

- Deliver accounts for 2003/04 that deliver cash targets
- Include management of cash shortfalls in financial recovery plans
- Comment on draft guidance

Quarter 2

- Present performance reports as required by SHA [R]

- Present plans to overcome unsupported cash shortfalls.

Quarter 4
- Agree financial plans for 2005/06.

4. Optimse NHS Estate

Aims to

- Ensure that the NHS estate is used effectively
- Sell sites that are surplus to requirement to avoid the unnecessary capital costs of holding estate that is surplus to requirements
- Generate capital receipts to contribute to the cash management strategy
- Address backlog maintenance to optimise the balance between maintenance costs and replace / refurbishment.

Delivery Targets

2003/04
Developed a methodology for reviewing the current estate in Surrey and Sussex to:

- Identify NHS land and buildings within each LHSCC and current values
- Identify current use and level of utilisation
- Establish long term plan for each site/building
- Identify land and buildings which are surplus to requirements or likely to become so
- Establish potential for improving utilisation and/or rationalising the existing estate
- Identify the potential for site disposals and related capital receipts.

2004/05 as above plus:
- Establish the current condition of the NHS estate and related backlog maintenance
- Carry out a review of the current estate and identify land and property surplus to requirements
- Develop a programme of estates optimisation and site disposal to reduce the cost of holding and maintaining real estate and to produce a stream of capital receipts to underpin financial recovery

- Ensure that backlog maintenance is a priority for investment from operational capital in the LDP.

2005/06

- Implement the programme of estates optimisation and site disposal strategy.

Risks to Delivery

- Lack of professional estates capacity within PCTs and trusts
- Lack of robust information.

Key Strengths

- Experience and expertise within NHS estates
- Potential for generating significant capital receipts.

SHA Enabling Strategies

- Transforming health and social care
- Capital investment strategy
- Training and development programme
- Performance management strategy.

Trusts' Delivery Plans

- PCT and trust estates strategies
- Capacity plans.

Actions for 2004/05

Note [R] denotes repeat each quarter

Strategic Health Authority (SHA)

Quarter 1
- Formalise the estates rationalisation methodology and issue guidance

- Agree project plan and set up project structure
- Acquire financial support
- Deliver workshop - improving financial health
- Draft SHA estates strategy including priority of schemes.

Quarter 2

- Evaluate estate strategies and provide recommendation to PCTs and trusts to optimise estate
- Validate performance reports against plans. Convene performance management meetings with PCTs and trusts. Report performance and present recommendations. [R]

Quarter 3

(See [R])

Quarter 4

- Manage delivery of performance targets
- Validate plans for 2005/06.

PCTs and Trusts

Quarter 1

- Confirm local delivery plans, service level agreements, source and application of funds, investment and financial recovery plans, risk management strategies and contingency plans
- Deliver unqualified accounts for 2003/04 and statements of internal control
- Update or confirm estates strategies.

Quarter 2

- Present performance reports as required by SHA. [R]

Quarter 3

(See [R])

Quarter 4

- Set plans for 2005/06.

5. Productivity/Efficiency - Back Office Functions

Aims to

- Review the scope and opportunity for shared service arrangements and outsourcing
- Modernise procurement practices and processes to deliver more effective purchasing arrangements and significant non-pay savings.

Delivery Targets

2003/04

- Set up programme board to improve procurement and shared services.
- Identified the options for improving and rationalising financial services and other back office functions to produce increased efficiencies and more effective service provision.

2004/05 above plus:

- Agree strategy to standardise processes related to financial services
- Lead a programme of service improvement and rationalisation based on the Shared Services model
- Modernise procurement practices and processes and encourage a more collaborative approach to procurement in Surrey and Sussex to realise potential savings scoped at between 5% and 10% on current non-pay expenditure.

2005/06

- Deliver savings of £25m to be realised over the period 2004/05 to 2007/08 to underpin FRPs.

Risks to Delivery

- Lack of support at board level within NHS organisations
- Unwillingness of organisations to cede local autonomy
- NHS Trusts fail to participate in the supply confederations
- Lack of professional procurement expertise.

Key Strengths

- Enormous scope for generating savings without any adverse impact on service provision
- A number of supply managers committed to the confederation concept
- History and track record of collaborative purchasing in some parts of the health economy
- Support from the Purchasing and Supply Agency
- Opportunity to benefit from state of the art business systems.

SHA Enabling Strategies

- Financial Recovery Plans.

Trusts' Delivery Plans

- Financial Recovery Plans.

Actions for 2004/05

Note [R] denotes repeat each quarter

Strategic Health Authority (SHA)

Quarter 1
- Draft strategy
- Deliver workshop - improving productivity and efficiency in back office functions.

Quarter 2
- Confirm strategy and agree process of implementation.

Quarter 3
- Review progress against agreed plans. [R]

PCTs and Trusts

Quarter 1
- Respond to draft strategy.

Quarter 2
- Commence implementation of strategy.

Quarter 3
- Present performance reports as required by SHA. [R]

Quarter 4
- Agree plans for 2005/06.

6. Financial Flows/Payment by Results

Aims to

- Improve the efficiency and effectiveness of health service commissioning
- Implement plans to introduce payments by results (PbR)
- Assess and manage the risks to individual organisations.

Delivery Targets

PbR is a fundamental part of NHS modernisation and service improvement. Its introduction is necessary to support a devolved health system with care delivered by a diverse range of providers responding to patients' needs and choices.

Payment by results changes the way that healthcare providers will be paid by linking the flow of funds with activity. This new system:

- Pays NHS Trusts and other providers fairly and transparently for services and actual activity delivered
- Rewards efficiency and quality in providing services
- Supports greater patient choice and more responsive services

- Enables PCTs to concentrate on quality and quantity rather than price by setting standard national prices (adjusted for regional variations in cost) for clinical procedures.

In addition PbR should create incentives to increase elective activity and capacity, encourage plurality of provision through the use of the new independent sector provision and foundation hospitals and provide a mechanism to demonstrate how the new investment in the NHS is being used.

The plans will be introduced within a very tight framework. The changes will be partially implemented in 2003/04 and 2004/05, with full implementation in 2005/06. At this time the national tariff will be applied alongside a staged (three year) transition period until end 2007/08. Payment by Results using the National Tariff will be fully operational in 2008/9. [Note: The timetable has since changed - see www.dh.gov.uk for the latest position.]

PbR is a significant financial systems change within the NHS and will enable a number of other policy initiatives. These are incorporated in the key objectives below.

The precise scope of the new financial flow system is still being defined. The following key objectives, risks, targets and milestones have been based on the available information to date but will need to reviewed and updated as new guidance is issued.

Key Objectives and Targets

Key Objectives for Surrey and Sussex are:

- Ensure that all organisations are able to provide and commission services at national tariff rates in a financially sustainable way
- Ensure that all organisations in Surrey and Sussex are prepared for, and able to support, the new financial flows regime
- Assess the opportunities and risks to all organisations from the move to PbR and ensure that all organisations have strategies for managing and/or mitigating these risks.

Risks to Delivery

There are many risks associated with the delivery of PbR. The main ones are outlined below:

- Not seen as a total systems change - ie the clear links between the funding model, patient choice and service improvement is not established and communicated
- Not seen as requiring a cross-functional focus - i.e. clinicians and managers need to become part of the changes taking place, as much as finance, IT, contracting and commissioning staff
- Lack of engagement within organisations - initiative seen purely as a financial project
- There is insufficient time, skill and effort applied to prepare for the new system
- Commissioning has not developed sufficiently - for example, not able to commission at a C&V / HRG level
- Commissioners do not have sufficient skills and knowledge to undertake demand planning and capacity management in a systematic way to support the movement of activity between providers to allow for waiting targets and patient choice to be delivered (over-trading and excess demand)
- Commissioning on the basis of packages of care is discouraged as initial attention is focused on acute hospital procedures
- Information and financial systems are not in place to agree and monitor agreements at a C&V / HRG level
- Poor quality of clinical coding and data
- HRGs are not robust enough to be used to adjust funding to reflect the complexity of the actual caseload
- Providers are unable to make the annual efficiency gains to reduce their costs to national tariff levels
- Providers fail the 'going concern' test as their cost base is materially above the tariff income that its activities can generate
- Reference costs are not sufficiently accurate due to low quality costing information; high reference costs in some trusts
- The move from FCEs (finished consultant episodes) to spells may reduce the level of expected income to providers who have a high FCE: spell ratio.

Key Strengths

- Good relationships between PCTs and trusts
- Good linkages with the DH
- Cross organisational director level group focusing on the issues of implementing PbR
- Local health economy implementation groups
- Good knowledge of reference costs.

Enabling Strategies

These enabling strategies need to be implemented within each organisation to support the implementation of PbR:

- Costing (as NHS reference costs will be the starting point for the national tariff) - integrate costing into internal management processes within organisations
- Data quality and clinical coding (as payments will be made for known clinical activity)
- Budget management as part of the organisations' business planning and performance management processes (as budgets will need to be linked to activity and expected income based on the tariff)
- Systems - financial and information (as organisations will need to have the ability to set up and monitor the activity, costs and income in a more proactive, detailed manner). This needs to be linked to the strategic review of shared services
- Demand planning and management (as PCTs will need to understand the levels of activity to be commissioned from each provider to meet targets and patient choice)
- Capacity management (as providers will need to ensure that capacity is available to meet anticipated demand)
- Risk sharing (ensure risks are managed and where appropriate, shared)
- Commissioning (as commissioners will need to agree the appropriate care pathways and the expected quality standards and clinical outcomes).

Actions for 2004/05

There are many actions that need to take place to implement PbR. Below are the key milestones that need to be achieved during 2004/05.

Each trust / local health community will need to have a local plan for meeting these milestones within the appropriate timescale. A detailed implementation plan is being developed.

Strong, structured project management is required across Surrey and Sussex within each Trust / LHE / PCT to ensure implementation takes place. The structures should be agreed and in place by April 04.

The SHA is the conduit between the service and the centre. The SHA will be responsible for monitoring the implementation of PbR in each Trust / LHC / PCT. Assessment of readiness will need to take place formally at least every quarter - Jan 04/April 04/July 04/Oct 04

Note [R] denotes repeat each quarter

Strategic Health Authority (SHA)

Quarter 1
- Validate compliance with 2003/04 requirements - cost and volume agreements for a minimum of 6 specialties and HRG level agreements to 15 procedures
- Confirm improvement in clinical coding to the level required by PbR
- Confirm SLAs agreed in the form compliant with DH guidance
- Confirm calculation of reference costs materially accurate
- Deliver workshop - PbR
- Estimate financial risks of gaps between baseline funding and PbR national tariff
- Review DH guidance and advise PCTs and Trusts
- Confirm transitional arrangements with DH.

Quarter 2
- Confirm rebasing by PCTs and Trusts is in line with DH guidance and is materially accurate.

Quarter 3
- Advise and hold workshop to discuss the transitional arrangements set by the DH.

Quarter 4

- Evaluate and advise on financial plans for 2005/06.

PCTs and Trusts

Quarter 1

- Demonstrate compliance with 2003/04 requirements - cost and volume agreements for a minimum of 6 specialties and HRG level agreements to 15 procedures
- Demonstrate improvement in clinical coding to the level required by PbR
- Demonstrate SLAs agreed in the form compliant with DH guidance
- Confirm calculation of reference costs materially accurate
- Estimate financial risks of gaps between baseline funding and PbR national tariff
- Estimate financial risks arising from PbR and prepare a risk management strategy.

Quarter 2

- Carry out cost rebasing exercise in line with DH guidance
- Confirm tariffs issued by DH (Sep) are materially accurate.

Quarter 3

- Advise SHA of financial risks arising from transitional arrangements set by DH.

Quarter 4

- Agree financial plans for 2005/06 on the basis of PbR.

Appendix 2

Surrey and Sussex SHA: Template Health Community Financial Recovery Plan 2004/05 to 2007/08

1. Executive Summary

1.1 The [Trust/PCT] Board received, in [month, year] financial reports that predicted a deficit [or the risk of a deficit] of [£amount] contributing to a deficit of [£amount] for the Template Health Community. As a result of this the Board directed the Executive to prepare a Financial Recovery Plan.

1.2 This Financial Recovery Plan has been prepared as directed. It has been prepared in accordance with national and supplementary guidance from the Surrey and Sussex Strategic Health Authority.

1.3 This plan is yet to be agreed with the Surrey and Sussex Strategic Health Authority.

1.4 This recovery plan recovers the deficit position over the shortest possible period. All key stakeholders have agreed to this plan and both the NHS Trust and the host PCT have agreed how the deficit can be cash managed in the interim without breaching the public sector payments policy.

1.5 Specifically, this Financial Recovery Plan:

- Quantifies and explains the cause for the cumulative deficit of the NHS organisation in the context of the Template Health Community that is the baseline for 2005-8 planning
- Presents an agreed plan that shows how the underlying recurrent deficit is to be overcome to achieve a balanced position by the end of the planning period
- Demonstrates agreement between the following NHS organisations within the Template Health Community:
- Upper Template NHS Trust
- Lower Template NHS Trust
- Middle Template Community NHS Trust

- North Template PCT
- South Template PCT
- Template Local Authority.

1.6 Section 2 of this plan headed The Financial Problem defines the financial problem. It includes:

- A clear quantification of the size of the underlying financial problem separated by cause and whether these problems are recurrent or non-recurrent for each year in the planning period
- An assessment of the current and future trend of the problems i.e. whether the problem has stabilised, is growing or reducing
- Explanations of all material assumptions used.

1.7 Section 3 headed The Reason for the Deficit explains the cause of the financial problems so as to provide confidence that the remedies proposed are both appropriate and will be effective in restoring financial balance. The cause of the financial problems includes the following:

- Financial control issues
- Configuration issues (service and/or organisational)
- Activity and cost pressures
- General management issues
- The financial positions of commissioners.

1.8 Section 4, Action to Date, describes the measures/action taken to date to address the underlying recurrent financial problems, including an assessment of the effect of measures/action taken, for example:

- Savings plans, including the effect upon service levels, services generally, organisational changes, human resources etc
- Securing additional funds.

1.9 Section 5, Financial Recovery Plan, describes the measures planned (and agreed) to address the financial problems and restore the NHS Trust to a balanced financial position on a recurring basis and to effect the recovery of prior year deficits, including:

- Detailed savings plans
- Securing additional funds
- Service impact including service levels, waiting lists/times
- Organisational impact, including human resources, reconfigurations.

The above is quantified and profiled by year.

1.10 Section 6, Risk Analysis, provides an assessment of the risks associated with the delivery of the recovery plan, including:

- An assessment of the risks for each element of the recovery plan, including sensitivity and materiality
- Details of the contingency measures in place should any of the risks materialise.

1.11 Section 7, Cash Impact, provides an assessment of the cash impact of the financial problem, including:

- The NHS Trust's ability to meet its EFL and cash limit
- The restoration of cash and a 'healthy' balance sheet in the medium term
- The impact on working capital, restrictions on capital expenditure, sale of fixed assets etc
- Details of any brokerage agreed and the repayment requirements
- The above must be quantified and profiled by year (and preferably quarterly within year).

1.12 Section 8, Detail Reports, provides financial reports supporting the recovery plan that:

- Include an I&E account, balance sheet, EFL statement and a cash flow statement for the whole planning period
- Demonstrate that the NHS trust will return to an underlying financial balance by the end of the recovery period
- Show that the NHS trust is returned to a healthy cash position/balance sheet by the end of the recovery period.

1.13 Section 9, Control Environment, describes how progress against the recovery plan will be monitored, including:

- Written evidence of support from commissioner(s) & SHA's approval

- Clear milestones against which the implementation of the recovery plan will be measured and where intervention will be deemed necessary
- Details of performance management meetings (such as steering groups) involving the SHA, commissioner(s) and the NHS trust
- Nature and frequency of board level monitoring within the NHS trust.

2. The Financial Problem

2.1   As at December 2003 the Template Health Economy expects to carry forward to 2004/05 a reported outturn deficit of £5 million.

2.2   In 2003/04 £7 million of the Trusts' underlying deficit of £12 million were addressed non-recurrently and the capital to revenue transfers over the last 10 years has led to under investment in capital.

2.3   PCTs will report a balance this year. However, the full year effect of underlying cost pressures from prescribing, amounting to £3 million has been offset non-recurrently this year.

2.4   In 2004/05 the trusts' underlying deficit is expected to increase from £12 million to £15 million due to price increases and less effective infrastructure.

2.5   The PCTs' underlying deficit of £3 million will need to be addressed.

2.6   In total the local health community has a financial recovery target of £23 million for 2004/05.

2.7   In addition to this financial problem three of the key access targets are expected to be breached within the Template Health Community in the year ending 2003/04 and one of the NHS Trusts has a zero star rating.

2.8   Senior managers are citing poor financial management as cause for leaving in exit interviews and senior clinicians are refusing to attend any further meetings to discuss financial recovery.

2.9 Table 1, below, shows the size of the estimated underlying financial problem for 2004/05 by NHS organisation and expenditure type.

Table 1: Financial recovery target for the year ending March 2005 by NHS organisation and cost pressure.

£m	Upper T NHST	Lower T NHST	Middle T Com NHST	North T PCT	South T PCT
Carried forward	4.5	0.5			
Prescribing				2.0	1.0
Agency costs	4.0	2.2			
Pay > budget	1.5				
Drugs	1.0	0.2			
Clinical consumables	1.0	0.3			
Energy costs	0.5	0.3	1.0		
Infrastructure	1.0	0.5			
Price increases	1.5				
Total target	15.0	4.0	1.0	2.0	1.0

3. Reason for Deficits

3.1 This section explains the cause of the financial problems to demonstrate that the remedies proposed are both appropriate and will be effective in restoring financial balance.

3.2 The carried forward deficit

3.3 The prescribing deficits are due to

3.4 The agency costs

3.5 The pay costs

3.6 The clinical consumables

3.7 The energy costs

4.   Actions to Date

4.1   This section describes the impact of the measures/action taken to date to address the underlying recurrent financial problems.

4.2   This section describes the outcome of detailed assessments of the extent to which financial recovery schemes advised by the SHA may be applicable. A separate appendix is provided to the plan showing for each scheme whether the scheme has already been applied or is to be applied or is not applicable.

4.2   The underlying deficit for the Upper Template NHS Trust was reported to be £8 million in 2002/03 and this remains unchanged. The financial recovery plan agreed in 2002/03 has not delivered the cash releasing efficiency savings planned.

4.3   The underlying deficit for the Lower Template NHS Trust was reported to be £4 million in 2002/03 and this has reduced to £1 million, in 2003/04, due to the implementation of the financial recovery plan agreed in 2002/03, see appendix X.

4.4   The £3 million reduction in Lower Template deficit was due to:

- This,
- That, and
- The other thing.

5   Financial Recovery Plan 2005 - 2008

5.1   This section describes the agreed plans to address the financial problems and restore the NHS organisations within the Template Health Community to a balanced financial position on a recurring basis and to achieve the recovery of prior year deficits.

5.2   The FRP is summarised below with references to detailed explanations as to how the plan will be delivered.

Table 2: Plan to achieve financial recovery target.

£m	Note	Upper T NHST	Lower T NHST	Middle T Com NHST	North T PCT	South T PCT
Demand Mgt	5.3					
Infrastructure	5.4				2.0	1.0
Productivity	5.5	1.0	0.2			
D T of care	5.6	3.5				
Reduce costs	5.7	1.0	0.2			
Fin Mgt & Control	5.8	2.0	0.3			
Total target		12.5	1.5	1.0	2.0	1.0

5.3 Demand management

Annex A and B shows the strategic recovery plans and detail action plans agreed to deliver improved demand management. These measures will avoid unplanned development and reduce inappropriate use of health services, reprioritise provision of lower priority services and optimise supply of services within existing resources.

The key actions being taken include:

- This
- That and
- The other thing.

5.4 Infrastructure

Annex A and B shows the measures designed to optimise physical capacity so that it enables the best delivery of the optimum level of services.

The key actions being taken include:

- This
- That and
- The other thing.

5.5 Productivity

Annex A and B shows the measures designed to identify opportunities for improved productivity through improved clinical systems and service design.

The key actions being taken include:

- This
- That and
- The other thing.

5.6 Delayed transfers of care

Annex A and B shows the measures designed to reduced delayed transfers of care.

The key actions being taken include:

- This
- That and
- The other thing.

5.7 Reduce net costs

Annex A and B shows the measures designed to reduce net costs including improved human resource management, procurement, income generation and accounting practices.

The key actions being taken include:

- This
- That and
- The other thing.

5.8 Financial management and control

Annex A and B shows the measures designed to improve compliance with systems reflecting best practice in financial management and control.

The key actions being taken include:

- This
- That and
- The other thing.

6 Risk Analysis and Management

6.1 This section provides an assessment of the risks associated with the delivery of the recovery plan, including:

- An assessment of the risks for each element of the recovery plan, including sensitivity and materiality
- Details of the contingency measures in place should any of the risks materialise.

6.2 Annex B section D details the risks associated with the delivery of financial recovery plans.

6.3 The remainder of this part describes the agreed risk management strategy that has been designed to limit the negative impact of these risks and pro-actively address new risks as they arise.

6.4 The key aspects of the risk management strategy include:

- This,
- That and
- The other things.

7 Cash Impact

7.1 This section provides an assessment of the cash impact of the financial problem, including:

- The NHS trust's ability to meet its EFL and cash limit
- How any in year cash deficit will be managed in the short term
- The restoration of cash and a 'healthy' balance sheet in the medium term
- The impact on working capital, restrictions on capital expenditure, sale of fixed assets etc

- Details of any brokerage agreed and the repayment requirements

The above must be quantified and profiled by year (and preferably quarterly within year).

8 Detail Reports

8.1 This section provides financial reports supporting the recovery plan that:

- Include an I&E account, balance sheet, EFL statement and a cash flow statement for the whole planning period
- Demonstrate that the NHS trust will return to an underlying financial balance by the end of the recovery period.

9 Control Environment

9.1 This section describes how progress against the recovery plan will be controlled, including:

- Written evidence of support from commissioner(s) and SHA approval
- Clear milestones against which the implementation of the recovery plan will be measured and where intervention will be deemed necessary
- Details of performance management meetings (such as steering groups) involving the SHA, commissioner(s) and the NHS trust
- Nature and frequency of board level monitoring within the NHS trust.

ANNEX A CHECKLIST

The directors of finance and accountable officers of the following NHS organisations within the Template Health Community agree that they satisfy all applicable checklist items, except for the following:

This part describes the characteristics of organisational policy and corporate governance that will help deliver improved financial performance. The key characteristics are as follows:

SHA checklist items:	State, not applicable, fully implemented or actions being taken to implement.

Annex B

Financial Recovery Plans for 2004/05:
Strategic View of Financial Recovery Plans :

(all £ figures in thousands)

Work Stream:	Project Number:	Project Title:	Link project:	Project Lead:	Start Date:	End Date:	Capital resource required	Non-recurrent revenue required	Non-recurrent revenue saved	Net non-recurrent savings	Recurrent revenue required	Recurrent revenue saved	Net recurrent savings	Type 1	Type 2	Type 3	Net recurrent savings less risk
		Project:							Net Savings					Less Risks:			Equals
Strategy 1: Demand Mgt	1.1																
	1.2																
	1.3																
	Savings from demand management:																
Strategy 2: Infrastructure	2.1																
	2.2																
	2.3																
	Savings from improved infrastructure:																
Strategy 3: Productivity	3.1																
	3.2																
	3.3																
	Savings from optimised productivity:																
Strategy 4: DT of Care	4.1																
	4.2																
	4.3																
	Savings from less delayed transfers of care:																
Strategy 5: Financial Mgt and Control and reduce net costs	5.1																
	5.2																
	5.3																
	Savings from financial mgt and control:																
	Total savings:																

Financial Recovery Plan
Project Specification: Level 2
    Section A:

Work Stream:	
Project Number:	
Version:	
Project Title :	
Project Lead and Team:	

Section B:

	Design	Development	Implementation	Milestone
	�	☐	☐	●

		FY05 (ending 31 March 2005)				
Mth	Activity or Milestone	Q1	Q2	Q3	Q4	FY05	FY06

Section C:
ESTIMATED FINANCIAL impact for this project in £'000s
Keep separate notes about how the cost and benefits figures were arrived at.
Enter '-' for savings. Positive numbers represent additional costs:

Financial Impact	FY05 (yr end 31 March 2005)					
	05 Q1	05 Q2	05 Q3	05 Q4	FY05	FY06
Capital resource required						
This and that						
Non-recurrent revenue required						
This						
and that						
Non-recurrent revenue saving						
This						
and that						
Net non-recurrent savings						
Recurrent revenue required						
This						
That						
and the other thing						
Recurrent revenue saved						
This						
That						
and the other thing						
Net recurrent savings						

Less Risks (see Section D)						

Net recurrent savings less risk						

Section D: RISKS:

1	Type 1			
1.1	Description of risk	Impact	Probability	£ Risk

2	Type 2			
2.1	Description of risk	Impact	Probability	£ Risk

3	Type 3			
3.1	Description of risk	Impact	Probability	£ Risk

4	Type 4			
4.1	Description of risk	Impact	Probability	£ Risk

5	Type 5			
5.1	Description of risk	Impact	Probability	£ Risk

Total risk	

Financial Recovery Plan

Work Stream:

Project Number:

Version:

Project Title :

Project Lead and Team:

Record of Delivery

	Milestone per L2	Performance and Comments
April		
May		
June		
July		
August		
September		
October		
November		
December		
January		
Febuary		
March		

Hampshire and the Isle of Wight SHA: Checklist Template

Organisation name:

Recovery plan scheme checklist item	Action taken
1 **Pay**	
1.1 Reduction of absenteeism through improved information, tighter policy and management.	
1.2 Reduction in agency costs through the use of medical locums and nursing/A&C/AHP pool staff (use of NHSP) - good locum planning for annual leave/study leave.	
1.3 Minimise staff turnover.	
1.4 Improved efficiency of nursing staff establishment ratios through ward skill mix review - the optimum application of staff to meet service demand.	
1.5 Closer matching of staff competencies and capacity to service demand - skill mix appropriate to service.	
1.6 Use vacancies as an opportunity to recruit more efficient skill mix.	
1.7 Review management costs in line with health economy requirement to share resources.	
1.8 Efficient use of advertising for recruitment i.e. joint adverts.	
1.9 No appointments are made unless there is an appropriate vacant funded post. Budget holders may only appoint to vacant establishment posts.	
1.10 Reduction in agency costs through the NHS Professionals initiative.	
2 **Consumables and Services**	
2.1 Any development in clinical practice that has a material resource implication is approved by an appropriate	

executive clinical committee and the development does not take place until approval is give to the clinical aspects and a budget change is approved by the Accountable Officer on the recommendation of the Director of Finance.

2.2   Procurement processes comply with best practice.

2.3   Changes to clinical consumables are agreed by clinical products committee.

2.4   Reduced price / unit cost through PASA collaborative procurement initiative, new national contracts, and reverse auctioning.

2.5   Benchmark prices.

2.6   Improved energy price.

2.7   Improved energy efficiency.

2.8   Re-tendering supply and service contracts.

2.9   All early payment discounts are received.

2.10   Regular review of development of clinical protocols regarding the use of clinical consumables.

2.11   Note and minimise all stock disposals.

2.12   Note and minimise wastage.

2.13   Ensure clinical staff are aware of the cost of products (i.e. coloured labels on expensive items)

2.14   Review of training to ensure necessary to role.

2.15   Review of utility functions (water, gas, electric, oil, sewage, phones etc) to ensure competitive rates.

2.16   Review of welfare foods to ensure NHS only providing food to those entitled.

2.17   Review of maintenance contracts (estates, equipment, computers etc).

3   **Cost of Rates and Taxes**

3.1   Ensure contracts are tax and NI efficient i.e. nurseries, computers, lease cars etc

3.2   VAT rebates and VAT planning for investments i.e. VAT reviews by organisations such as VAT Liaison.

3.3   Appeal excessive rate revaluations.

4   **Prescribing**

4.1   Development of limited formulary.

4.2   Adherence to formulary.

4.3   Note and review of wastage.

4.4   Improve interface between primary and secondary care - to ensure drugs not prescribed twice, i.e. development of joint formularies.

4.5   Develop incentive schemes that reduce costs.

4.6   Use Audit Commission review to reduce costs.

4.7   Agreement on prescribing between hospitals and GPs to minimise the cost to the local health community.

4.8   Review practice prescribing data for outliers.

5   **Cost of Capital**

5.1   Sale of surplus estate and reduction in capital charge/running costs.

5.2   Optimal use of assets such as MRIs.

5.3   Managed services agreement for equipment.

5.4   Planned asset replacement programme to optimise maintenance costs compared with asset replacement.

5.5   Asset control to minimise losses.

5.6   Reclassification, review of lives, revaluation of assets to minimise capital charges.

5.7   Ensure any investment contributes to revenue savings.

5.8   Minimise the revenue consequences of 'new' capital.

5.9   Ensure donated assets are accurately recorded.

5.10   Ensure all expenditure that is possible is capitalised i.e. IT.

5.11   Sale and leaseback of assets.

6   Accounting Treatment

6.1   Correct overstatement of opening creditors and provisions.

6.2   Ensure year-end accruals are not overstated.

6.3   Correct overstated capital charges.

7   Income Generation

7.1   Maximise income from RTA charges.

7.2   Ensure OATs are correctly recorded to maximise future income and validated by PCTs.

7.3   Car parking charges.

7.4   Promotion of charitable support.

7.5   Ensure bids are lodged for all available funds.

7.6   Sale of legal charges over property.

7.7   Maximise income from:
- Private patients
- Coroners and post mortem examinations
- Dental services
- Walk-in centres
- Drugs/pharmacy services
- Pathololology services
- Diagnostic imaging capacity

- Laundry/hotel services
- Franchises for telephones/televisions
- Beverages/meals sold to visitors
- Payphones
- Baby scan photos
- Advertising space around the site/in directories.

7.8   Obtain sponsorship.

7.9   Ensure income from royalties is maximised.

7.10   Ensure income from research is maximised.

7.11   Ensure rents due are invoiced and terms reviewed on
        a regular basis.

7.12   Advertise and sell conference centre space.

7.13   Charge consultants for use of NHS premises, stock etc
        for private work.

7.14   Ensure all other rechargeable expenditure (charitable,
        NHSLA etc) is charged to the relevant organisation on
        a regular basis.

7.15   Sale of NHS occupational health services to the
        private sector.

7.16   NHS exploitation of intellectual property.
        (Awaiting legislation).

8   Service Redesign

8.1   Use of Modernisation Agency's 10 High
        Impact Changes.

8.2   Benchmark care pathways and services such as same
        day surgery against top quartile performing NHS
        organisations to identify and implement opportunities
        for improvement.

8.3   Reconfigure services to improve the value for money
        of pathology services, small specialties, sterile
        services and other clinical and non-clinical services
        currently provided on separate sites within the local
        health community.

8.4   Amalgamate services, such as ICU, ITU and Cardiac services to improve the value for money of services provided within an NHS organisation.

8.5   Improve service adjacencies, in areas such as theatre and A/E, to optimise the patient journey.

8.6   Manage elective admissions to enable the use of a weekday ward and reduce weekend working.

8.7   Benchmark clinical output, in areas such as theatre, against top quartile performers and identify and implement opportunities for improved efficiency through the automation of manual processes and improved scheduling of workload.

8.8   Review readmission rates and iatrogenic illness and identify and implement opportunities to reduce both.

8.9   Review and apply lessons learned by similar organisations that have invested in service redesign to improve efficiency.

8.10 Explore a section 31 partnership to improve partnership working and reduce bed blocking.

8.11 Develop interagency patient care planning and joint working to reduce bed blocking.

8.12 Establish admissions criteria to reduce inappropriate admissions.

8.13 Redesign inter-boundary referrals.

8.14 Develop shared services and review their cost effectiveness.

8.15 Develop, implement and update prescribing protocols and protocols for the use of diagnostic and clinical support services in hospitals.

8.16 Review and implement clinical audit initiatives that contribute to improved financial performance.

8.17 Review and implement improvements in information systems that contribute to improved financial performance.

8.18   Carry out capacity utilisation reviews to identify sub optimum use of capacity.

8.19   Consider the use of nurse practitioners.

8.20   Consider the development of a pre-admission clinic.

8.21   Consider the development of an acute assessment unit and fast track diagnosis to avoid unnecessary admissions.

8.22   Log and minimise all disruptions to service continuity from such things as stockouts, staff unavailability and infection.

8.23   Provide consultants each month with confidential personal productivity reports showing average productivity of consultants treating a comparable casemix.

8.24   Utilise patient hotel facilities rather than an inpatient bed where the patient does not require admission.

8.25   Use HRG reference cost benchmarking data.

8.26   Establish referral criteria to ensure no inappropriate referrals.

8.27   Review LOS.

8.28   Review of discharge arrangements.

8.29   The optimum application of staff and other resources to service demand. (ie Nurse rostering and theatre management systems)

9   Commissioning

9.1   Review services commissioned.

9.2   Review commissioning arrangements with the private sector.

9.3   Ensure section 28a arrangements are robust.

9.4   Ensure efficient use of special/mainland placements.

9.5   Ensure commissioning arrangements surrounding
       the nGMS contract are robust and represent value
       for money.

9.6   Management of referrals.

9.10   Review continuing care arrangements to ensure care
       packages are appropriately commissioned.

Appendix 3

Surrey and Sussex SHA: Register of Financial Recovery Schemes

This appendix sets out a series of financial recovery schemes that are designed to:

- Prioritise met demand through improved demand management
- Develop best fit infrastructure
- Optimise productivity / effectiveness
- Reduce delayed transfers
- Reduce net cost and avoid unaffordable new costs.

This register has been developed by Surrey and Sussex SHA and is continually updated and extended.

1. Demand Management

Supply demand modelling	Service supply and demand modelling and trend analysis identifies and helps avoid unplanned change in supply, demand and patients waiting by major specialty.
Applicable to	All organisations.
How will it help recovery?	Material increases in met demand will be controlled to the level that has demonstrated justification for its priority development, within affordability limits, relative to other services.
Evident by	Supply demand modelling and active prioritisation within affordability limits is evident. The justification of material increases in planned met demand is demonstrated. Unplanned developments of service are avoided.
Reference	DH capacity planning programme

Notes: Knowledge of year on year opening and closing waiting list numbers together with total and changes in supply and demand for each major service will inform capacity management decisions. This is closely related to needs analysis - see the infrastructure section of the register.

Zero based needs analysis	Individual services within local health communities are subject to zero based needs analysis by the commissioners and providers of the service at least once every four years. Supply of demand (met demand) for individual services will be examined and the rebalancing or cessation of individual service will be considered where patient benefits are deemed lowest. More cost effective ways of meeting acknowledged needs will be considered.
Applicable to	All organisations.
How will it help recovery?	The cost of services with the lowest benefit to patients will be saved or redeployed to higher patient priorities.
Evident by	A system of continual zero based needs analysis is evident. Accepted recommendations are implemented and result in planned improvement in value for patients.
Ambulance delivery to accident and emergency department	There are many occasions when patients are taken to A&E because there are no real alternatives.
Applicable to	Mainly PCTs and Ambulance Trusts.
How will it help recovery?	Reduced demand on A&E services and consequent reduction in inappropriate admissions.
Evident by	Reduced A&E attendances.

Needs analysis	Epidemiological analysis and benchmarking using clinical standards enables comparison between optimal mix and volume of service and current met demand (services supplied).
Applicable to	All organisations.
How will it help recovery?	Material increases in met demand will be controlled to the level that has demonstrated justification for its priority development, within affordability limits, relative to other services.
Evident by	Supply demand modelling and active prioritisation within affordability limits is evident. The justification of material increases in planned met demand is demonstrated.
Reference	DH capacity planning programme.

Note: A key early step in demand management should be to understand what optimal met demand looks like.

Clinical services review	Comprehensive clinical services review - to optimise the balance between different services supplied to meet demand within individual local health communities.
Applicable to	All organisations.
How will it help recovery?	Where appropriate, more cost effective services such as social care and community health care will substitute for more costly institutionalised care.
Evident by	Comprehensive review demonstrated. Accepted recommendations are implemented and result in planned improvement in value for patients.

Note: This is an exercise usually limited to a geographical area approximating a catchment area for one or two acute hospitals and related services.

Case management	Individual patients with a history of repeat emergency admissions to acute hospitals are personally managed to ensure they receive the most appropriate treatment and care in the most appropriate setting.
Applicable to	Mainly NHS trusts.
How will it help recovery?	Inappropriate emergency admissions and delayed discharges will be reduced.
Evident by	Existence of a case management system and evidence of reduction in inappropriate emergency admissions.
Reference	Kaiser Permanente; Evercare
GPs referral for tests & OPs	GP referrals to consultant outpatient clinics and direct referrals for diagnostic tests are subject to review and opportunities to optimise appropriateness of referrals. These reviews may be by sampling of individual case or analytical review of referrals compared with the pharmacy age sex and temporary resident adjusted prescribing unit.
Applicable to	PCTs.
How will it help recovery?	Inappropriate referrals and admissions will be reduced.
Evident by	Case reviews system is set up and anonymised findings are regularly published. Unnecessary referrals reduce.

Appropriateness evaluation Protocol (AEP)	Evaluate the appropriateness of hospital admissions with a view to reducing inappropriate admissions.
Applicable to	All organisations.
How will it help recovery?	Unnecessary admissions should be avoided enabling increased productivity for the same resources or reduced costs.
Evident by	AEP study carried out and accepted recommendations implemented. Baseline inappropriate admissions are reduced.
GPs referral for admission	Establish controls over GPs' directly arranging admission for their patients. All such referrals should be reviewed by A/E and referred to medical or surgical assessment units (MAU/ SAU).
Applicable to	All organisations.
How will it help recovery?	Unnecessary admissions and delayed discharges will be reduced and length of stay optimised.
Evident by	Agreed control systems involving A&E, MAU and SAU are evident. Unnecessary admissions and delayed discharges reduce.
Reduce re-admissions	Review causes of readmissions and implement opportunities to reduce readmission rates.
Applicable to	All organisations.
How will it help recovery?	Avoidable demand for admissions will be reduced.

Evident by	Reviews carried out and recommendations accepted. Accepted recommendations are implemented and deliver benefits.
Nurse practitioners	Consider the use of nurse practitioners in nurse led clinics.
Applicable to	Mainly NHS trusts.
How will it help recovery?	Services provided by nurse practitioners will substitute for consultant services enabling a net reduction in demand for more expensive services.
Evident by	Opportunities to establish nurse lead clinics reviewed. Accepted recommendations implemented.
Minor injuries unit (MIU)	Consider the use of GPs in MIU.
Applicable to	All organisations.
How will it help recovery?	Services provided by GPs will substitute for consultant lead A&E services enabling a net reduction in demand for more expensive services.
Evident by	Opportunities to MIUs reviewed. Accepted recommendations implemented
Pre-admission clinic	Consider the development of a pre-admission clinic to work up information required for elective surgery to avoid unnecessary admission of elective patients the day before surgery.
Applicable to	Mainly NHS trusts.
How will it help recovery?	Patients who cannot be treated within 24 hours of admission will not be admitted

and arrangements will be made for patients discharge to avoid delayed transfers.

Referral protocols and development

Agree referral protocols to guide GP referrals to outpatient clinics, diagnostic and allied health services. Patients needing prostheses could be referred directly to orthotists. GPs may refer patients to physiotherapist rather than orthopaedic surgeon.

Applicable to

All organisations.

How will it help recovery?

Unnecessary referrals are reduced.

Evident by

Protocols are agreed and are complied with. Referrals reduce.

Admissions criteria and development

Establish admissions criteria to reduce inappropriate admissions by phone call between GPs and on-call Registrars.

Applicable to

All organisations.

How will it help recovery?

Inappropriate admissions will be reduced.

Evident by

Protocols are agreed and are complied with. Inappropriate admissions reduce as evidenced by post implementation study.

Prescribing protocol and development

Develop, implement and update prescribing protocols for GPs and acute care. Formulary.

Applicable to

All organisations.

How will it help recovery?

Prescribing will optimise patient care and cost.

Evident by

Existence of protocol and lower than

	average prescribing costs and or reduction in cost per ASTRO PU.
Reference	PPA
Pathology protocols and development	Develop, implement and update protocols for the use of pathology services in hospitals.
Applicable to	Mainly NHS trusts.
How will it help recovery?	The costs of providing inappropriate tests will be reduced.
Evident by	Agreed protocols are complied with. reduction in inappropriate tests evident from post implementation study.
Radiology protocols and development	Develop, implement and update protocols for the use of radiology services in hospitals.
Applicable to	Mainly NHS trusts.
How will it help recovery?	The costs of providing inappropriate tests will be reduced.
Evident by	Agreed protocols are complied with. Reduction in inappropriate tests evident from post implementation study.
On call arrangements	Review all on call arrangements to assess whether alternative delivery models may reduce costs, i.e. 24 hour working or extended shift patterns.
Applicable to	Mainly NHS trusts.
How will it help recovery?	Reduced costs of service delivery, cap further increases.

Evident by	Papers to the clinical directorates and /or executive detailing and costing alternative service delivery models.
Protocol for referral to allied health services and development	Develop, implement and update protocols for the use of allied health services.
Applicable to	All organisations.
How will it help recovery?	Reduce unnecessary referrals and also substitute referrals to consultants' outpatient clinics.
Evident by	Agreed protocols are complied with. Reduction in inappropriate tests evident from post implementation study.

2. Infrastructure

Strategic fit - infrastructure	Through service supply and demand modelling and strategic analysis identify opportunities to improve strategic fit of infrastructure and match capacity with long term demand ensuring that any increase in capacity to meet demand is justified - i.e. long term capacity is not being developed to match short term demand and increased demand is justified by needs and affordability analysis.
Applicable to	All organisations.
How will it help recovery?	Optimum configuration of service infrastructure will increase productivity, improve flexibility in supply and save costs by reducing the number of less cost effective smaller acute hospitals duplicating

services, and improving the balance between specialist and acute treatment facilities, treatment centres, outreach clinics, intermediate and primary care support and home help. Development of acute bed capacity when new treatment regimes are reducing length of stay will also be avoided.

Compliance	Systems exist to ensure Transforming Health and Social Care Strategy, Capacity Plans, Estates Strategies and Investment Plans within Local Health Communities include plans to deliver optimum strategic configuration of health and social care service infrastructure and achieve quantified benefits. Agreed plans are supported by agreed detail implementation plans.
Validation	Agreed integrated plans are being implemented and are delivering increased productivity and savings.
Key milestones to delivery	LHCs agree integrated plans and agreements including capacity plans, estates strategies and investment programme to optimise strategic configuration of health and social care infrastructure. SHAs confirm priority using agreed prioritisation criteria agreed by the capital investment team. LHCs agree detail plans to implement investment programme. Implement investment programme. Term: 3 to 5 years
Capacity Rationalisation	Capacity is configured to optimise the provision of pathology services, small specialities, sterile services and other clinical and non-clinical services currently

	provided on separate sites within the local health community.
Applicable to	Mainly NHS trusts.
How will it help recovery?	Economies of scale may be achieved from centralised services.
Evident by	Evidence of recent evaluation of opportunities to rationalise capacity and recommendation of improvement. Recent recommendations to rationalise capacity are implemented and benefits realised.
Reference	Hammersmith project
s31 Partnerships	Explore inter-agency section 31 partnerships to improve partnership working and reduce bed-blocking arising from delayed transfers of patients out of acute hospitals.
Applicable to	All organisations.
How will it help recovery?	Risk sharing between social services and the NHS may result in improved co- ordination of services reducing delay in patient transfers between agencies.
Evident by	Opportunities for s31 partnerships are explored and value for money proposals are accepted. VFM proposals are implemented delivering reduced delayed transfers between agencies.
Optimise inter-boundary referrals	Identify sub-optimal inter-boundary referrals for specialist treatment and repatriate patients by creating new specialist centres, expand specialist units, or outreach clinics that can better treat patients closer to home.

Applicable to	All organisations.
How will it help recovery?	Marginal cost saving from patients currently being treated in more expensive specialist hospitals out of area.
Evident by	Opportunities for patient repatriation are explored and VFM proposals are implemented resulting in reduced net cost of services.
Reference	Maidstone and Brighton cancer centres.
Clinical Adjacencies Review	Capacity is configured to optimise clinical adjacencies of ICU, HDU and Cardiac, A&E and theatres services to improve the VFM of services provided within an NHS organisation.
Applicable to	All organisations.
How will it help recovery?	Improved productivity should substitute for increased costs.
Evident by	Comprehensive review of clinical adjacencies is demonstrated. Accepted recommendations are implemented and result in delivery of planned benefits.
Reference	Lewisham hospital reconfiguration.
Develop shared services	Develop shared services in clinical support and administrative functions.
Applicable to	All organisations.
How will it help recovery?	Economies of scale and levelling up best practice should increase productivity and reduce costs.

Evident by

Proper review of opportunities available through shared services is demonstrated. Accepted proposals are implemented and deliver benefits.

3. Optimise productivity / effectiveness

Analysis of average length of stay (ALOS), delayed transfers and delays evident in study of medical records together with comparison of clinical systems with evidenced based optima will identify opportunities for improved productivity through improved clinical systems and service design. These opportunities should be tested and if proved should be agreed, planned and implemented and complied with.

Service systems re-design

Change service systems design in line with best practice.

Applicable to

All organisations.

How will it help recovery?

Increased productivity can substitute for increased cost of buying additional activity.

Evident by

Systematic evaluation of clinical services results in clinical agreement to a documented plan or plans to improve clinical systems. These systems are demonstrably in line with (evidence based) optimum clinical systems that have been documented and approved by Medical Advisory Group or similar. Clinicians understand the systems and protocols they have agreed to apply. Clinicians receive regular reports on their performance compared with systems and output agreements. Clinicians receive support from clinical case managers who advise on patients' progress through agreed care pathways. Clinicians receive support from senior Physician Advisor on

compliance with systems and
performance norms.

Reference	South Yorkshire orthopaedics
Performance and reward management	Clinical performance related to reward package.
Applicable to	Mainly NHS trusts.
How will it help recovery?	Improved productivity avoids increased costs.
Evident by	Clinical contracts that enable clear performance target setting for clinicians and management of performance to target. i.e. consultant contract work plans.
Capacity utilisation review - macro	Carry out capacity utilisation reviews to identify sub optimum use of total physical capacity of A&E, theatres, pathology, radiology and wards. Key clinical performance indicators are available from collaborative groups such as TARN for A&E.
Applicable to	Mainly NHS trusts.
How will it help recovery?	Under utilised resources will be employed and over utilised capacity restricting flexibility to manage patients efficiently will be addressed.
Evident by	Capacity utilisation review demonstrated. Accepted recommendations are implemented and result in improved productivity.
Optimise use of surplus assets	Identify, declare, sell or redeploy surplus estate.

Applicable to	All organisations.
How will it help recovery?	Reduced capital charges and related costs and profit on sale of surplus property should save revenue and sale proceeds will improve cash liquidity.
Evident by	Comprehensive review led by NHS Estates demonstrated. Accepted recommendations are implemented and result in planned reduction in capital costs relative to similar acute services.
Optimise equipment use	Carry out review, informed by delays and critical path analysis and ALOS, to identify sub-optimal availability and use of pathology equipment and other diagnostic tools such as MRIs.
Applicable to	Mainly NHS trusts.
How will it help recovery?	Improved productivity should substitute for increased cost of increased services.
Evident by	Review led by clinicians using equipment is demonstrated. Accepted recommendations are implemented and result in planned reduction in delays in patient treatment.
Invest to improve productivity	Invite and evaluate opportunities to improve productivity and reduce costs through investment in better equipment enabling automation of some procedures.
Applicable to	Mainly NHS trusts.
How will it help recovery?	Investment focussed on improved productivity and cost effectiveness should reduce cost or improve productivity and also motivate key staff.

Evident by	Clinicians are given the opportunity to bid for investment where they can demonstrate that such investment would deliver improved productivity and cost effectiveness. Bids presenting value for money are accepted and implemented. Implemented schemes deliver planned benefits.
Information systems	Review and implement opportunities arising from the national procurement programme and local strategic capital investment as well as local investment to deliver improvements in information systems that support analysis of care pathways and performance assessment or directly contribute to improved productivity and or financial performance.
Applicable to	All organisations.
How will it help recovery?	Improved productivity will substitute for increased cost of buying additional services.
Evident by	Review and follow up action is demonstrated. Accepted recommendations are implemented and result in planned improvement in value for patients.
Theatre management system	The optimum application of theatre resources to service demand. (i.e. theatre management systems)
Applicable to	Mainly NHS trusts.
How will it help recovery?	Should improve efficiency and reduce the need for agency staff.
Evident by	Computer assisted theatre management

system is in place. Reduction in agency requirements is evident.

Benchmark service mix

Benchmark the proportion of surgery and other procedures provided within same day facilities against top quartile performing NHS organisations to identify and implement opportunities for improvement.

Applicable to

Mainly NHS trusts.

How will it help recovery?

A better fit between resources applied and patient acuity will be achieved. Improved productivity will substitute for costs of increased services.

Evident by

Benchmarking analysis and follow up action is evident. Accepted recommendations are implemented and result in planned increase in same day surgery.

Benchmark intra hospital care pathways

For specialties with bottom quartile ALOS, review by sample of medical records individuals' care pathways and identify occasions of unnecessary delay. Expose departure from best practice to peer review and agree plans to develop best practice.Clinicians revise pathway protocols and promote compliance with best practice.

Applicable to

Mainly NHS trusts.

How will it help recovery?

Departures from optimal care pathways should be reduced, reducing patient length of stay and or unnecessary procedures.

Evident by

Care pathway analysis demonstrated and proposals for improvement are accepted.

Accepted proposals are implemented delivering reduced length of stay.

Weekday ward

Manage elective admissions to enable the use of a weekday ward and reduce weekend working.

Applicable to

Mainly NHS Trusts.

How will it help recovery?

Reduced cost of weekend working.

Evident by

Management of elective admissions complies with best practice. Weekend working is reduced.

Admissions management

Manage elective admissions to reduce delays caused by temporary demands on diagnostic services in excess of capacity.

Applicable to

NHS Trusts.

How will it help recovery?

Reduced delays caused by bottlenecks in diagnostic and therapeutic support.

Evident by

Management of elective admissions complying with best practice is evident. Delays in access to diagnostic and other support services are reduced.

Bed assignment to specialties - consultants

Analyse bed allocations to specialties and individual consultants using utilisation rates and ALOS figures to optimise allocation.

Applicable to

NHS Trusts.

How will it help recovery?

Opportunities to improve overall utilisation should improve productivity and avoid costs arising from increased activity.

Evident by

Reviews demonstrate allocation is optimised and that opportunities for improvement are agreed. Agreed opportunities are implemented and deliver planned benefits.

Patient streaming   Identify opportunities for improved efficiency in the provision of service through patient streaming informed by process re-engineering studies supported by the modernisation agency.

Applicable to   Mainly NHS Trusts.

How will it help recovery?   Increased productivity can substitute for increased cost of buying additional activity.

Evident by   Patient streaming evaluated and focussed process re-engineering exercises test current practice. Accepted recommendations are implemented and deliver benefits.

Productivity benchmarking   Benchmark clinical output, in areas such as theatre, against top quartile performers in similar organisations and identify and implement opportunities for improved efficiency through the automation of manual processes and improved scheduling of workload.

Applicable to   Mainly NHS Trusts.

How will it help recovery?   Increased productivity can substitute for increased cost of buying additional activity.

Evident by   Clinical output evaluated, opportunities for improvement identified and recommendations accepted. Accepted recommendations are implemented and deliver benefits.

Reduce iatrogenisis	Review readmission rates, incidence of iatrogenic illness and identify and implement opportunities to reduce both.
Applicable to	All organisations.
How will it help recovery?	Reduced avoidable demand and improved length of stay.
Evident by	Review carried out and recommendations accepted. Accepted recommendations are implemented and deliver reduced readmissions and length of stay.
Clinical audit	Review and implement clinical audit initiatives that contribute to improved clinical productivity and effectiveness.
Applicable to	All organisations.
How will it help recovery?	Clinical audit programme of studies is agreed by the Board - Medical Advisory Committee or similar. Outcomes including proposals arising from clinical audits are presented to the Committee. Anonymised studies are published / best practice shared.
Evident by	Uptake of clinical audit initiatives and improved productivity and cost reduction evident from post implementation review.
Reference	Royal Colleges clinical audit websites.
Personal performance reports	Provide consultants each month with confidential personal productivity reports showing average productivity of consultants treating a comparable case mix. Provide Trust medical directors with reports that identify performance outliers.

New consultant contract productivity plans. Compare individual performance against anonymised clinical performance information prepared and reported by the Royal College of Surgeons. Information may be available on the RCS website.

Applicable to   NHS Trusts.

How will it help recovery?   Consultants will be better informed regarding their performance relative to their peers.

Evident by   Reduction in outlier performance.

4. Reduce delayed transfers

Patient transfers to lower acuity setting

Quantify and identify reasons for delayed discharges and benchmark processes of discharge and inter-agency care planning and transfers against best practice.

Applicable to   All organisations.

How will it help recovery?   Patients who should be discharged to home (with care) or requiring lower acuity of treatment and nursing care or accommodation in residential care are not in hospital in areas resourced to manage patients needing higher acuity treatment and nursing care.

Evident by   Processes of discharge and inter-agency care planning and transfers reflect best practice. Sufficient intermediate care, nursing care, residential care, home help and aids and appliances and support to charitable organisations enable patient transfer from the acute care setting. The number of beds blocked due to delayed discharges to home is reducing. Also see MAU, SAU and pre-admission clinic.

Patient transfer to specialist hospital

Quantify delayed discharges and benchmark processes of discharge and inter-agency care planning and transfers against best practice.

Applicable to

All organisations.

How will it help recovery?

Patients who should be discharged to a specialist hospital are not unnecessarily occupying a hospital bed.

Evident by

Processes of discharge and inter-agency care planning and transfers reflect best practice. The number of beds blocked due to delayed transfers of care to specialist hospitals is reduced.

Medical and surgical assessment unit

Assign a ward MAU and or SAU with beds and ability to fast-track diagnosis, treatment and appropriate discharge. Discharge planning commences in the assessment unit.

Applicable to

NHS Trusts.

How will it help recovery?

This should avoid delays in discharging patients.

Extend pharmacy hours

Opening the pharmacy till later and having staff pattern changed to enable patients to be discharged later in the day.

Applicable to

Mainly NHS Trusts.

How will it help recovery?

Avoid unnecessary overnight stays when only reason for the patient remaining in the hospital is access to drugs.

Discharge policy   Agreed discharge policy applied.

Applicable to   All organisations.

How will it help recovery?   Delayed transfers of care reduced.

Home aids and appliances   Provided to repeat re-attendances.

Applicable to   Mainly PCTs.

How will it help recovery?   Avoidable admissions minimised.

Charity support   Joint projects financing charities to provide support services to enable earlier discharge of patients.

Applicable to   All organisations.

How will it help recovery?   Avoidable admissions minimised and delayed transfers of care reduced.

5. Reduce net costs

Human Resource Management

Staff establishment management   Budgets for pay agree to the staff **and** establishment register that shows the number and grade of staff employed is sufficient to achieve service requirements and is affordable.

Applicable to   All organisations.

How will it help recovery?   Appointments to established but unfunded posts should stop.

Evident by   The electronic staff record system developed through the national programme is integrated with the budgeting system. Staff budgets are not exceeded.

Reduction to staff establishment	As demand management begins to take effect there needs to be a systematic review of number of beds and wards required and subsequently the level of funded establishment.
Applicable to	All organisations.
How will it help recovery?	Reduction to funded establishment and consequently reduced need for agency staff.
Evident by	Reduced establishment, lower pay and agency costs.
Staff resourcing	The optimum application of staff and other resources to service demand. (i.e. nurse rosters and theatre management systems).
Applicable to	All organisations.
How will it help recovery?	Should improve efficiency and reduce the need for agency staff.
Evident by	Computer assisted acuity based clinical resourcing system is in place. Reduction in agency requirements is evident.
General appointments	No appointments are made unless there is an appropriate vacant funded post. Budget holders may only appoint to vacant establishment posts.
Applicable to	All organisations.
Consultant appointments	The executive should approve all appointments, even if there is an appropriate vacant funded post.
Applicable to	Mainly NHS Trusts.

How will it help recovery?	Gives opportunity to consider alternative grades, use of nurse consultants and joint working across sites.
Evident by	Reduced medical staffing costs and funded establishment.
Tendering for locums	Review audit commission recommendations and take appropriate action with tendering /controls with locums and medical posts.
Applicable to	All organisations.
Absenteeism	Reduction of absenteeism through improved information, benchmarking performance, tighter policy and management.
Applicable to	All organisations.
How will it help recovery?	Reduced absenteeism rates compared with like trusts.
Evident by	Compare absenteeism rates by organisation and identify outliers.
Agency costs	Reduction in agency costs through the use of medical locums and nursing pool staff.
Applicable to	All organisations
How will it help recovery?	Medical locums and nursing pool staff cost less than agency staff.
Evident by	Systems in place and % paid to agencies benchmarked against similar organisations.
Agency costs	Agree levels of agency usage 1 month in advance and control spending to

authorised limits, monitor against level. Providing reports to budget holders accountable.

Applicable to	All organisations
How will it help recovery?	Authorisation limits should reduce use and cost.
Agency costs	Implement the NHS professionals initiative or similar.
Applicable to	All organisations
How will it help recovery?	Reduction in agency costs.
Staff turnover	Minimisation of staff turnover through improved information, benchmarking performance, tighter policy and management.
Applicable to	All organisations
How will it help recovery?	Reduce direct cost of appointments and reduce disruption caused by high turnover.
Evident by	Benchmarked turnover rates.
Skill mix review	Improved efficiency of nursing staff establishment ratios through ward skill mix review.
Applicable to	All organisations
How will it help recovery?	Closer matching of staff competencies and capacity to service demand.
Evident by	Existence of current skills mix review upon which the staff establishment is based.
e-recruitment	National initiative

Applicable to	All organisations
How will it help recovery?	Reduce advertising costs improving recruitment practice
Evident by	Benchmarking advertising costs against similar organisations
Reference	http://www.jobs.nhs.uk/

6. Procurement

Procurement Strategy	The procurement strategy best fits the requirements of all NHS organisations in Surrey and Sussex. Procurement centralisation, collaboration or co-ordination strategy is agreed.
Procurement Capacity	Employ procurement specialists and modern procurement systems and practices.
Applicable to	Mainly NHS trusts.
Collective contracts	Collective contracts with private sector across organisations so that larger and longer-term contracts that reduce risk to suppliers should reduce cost to the buyer.
Applicable to	All organisations.
New product management	Changes to clinical consumables are agreed by clinical products committee.
Applicable to	Mainly NHS trusts.
Price benchmarking	Prices and unit costs are regularly compared between NHS organisations and lowest prices taken up.

Applicable to	Mainly NHS trusts.
Tender waivers	Audit tender waivers.
Applicable to	All organisations.
Benchmark energy prices	Improved energy price.
Applicable to	All organisations.
Market testing	Re-tendering supply and service contracts. Negotiate improved prices and improvements in service efficiency.
Applicable to	All organisations.
Early payment discounts	All early payment discounts are received.
Applicable to	All organisations.
GP Prescribing	Focus on individual GP practice on high cost, influential areas.
Applicable to	PCTs.
Value Added Tax	VAT rebates and VAT planning for investments.
Applicable to	All organisations.
Appeal rates	Appeal excessive rate revaluations.
Applicable to	All organisations.
Audit energy use	Benchmark energy usage against similar hospitals.
Applicable to	All organisations.
Telephone costs	Control use of mobile phones, blocking expensive numbers.

Applicable to	All organisations.
1st class mail	Should be restricted. Compare cost of mail as a proportion of total costs by organisation and identify outliers.
Applicable to	All organisations.
GP prescribing initiative	Develop, implement and update prescribing initiative for general practice to ensure coherence between SHA prescribing strategy and PCTs operational action plans. Compare costs per ASTRO PU by GP and identify outliers. Understand reasons for outlying costs.Identify opportunities to improve cost effectiveness Prepare and implement plan. Evident decrease in costs to bottom quartile levels nationally.
Applicable to	PCTs.
Protocols	Develop protocols regarding the use of clinical consumables and monitor use against protocols. Identify outlier practice and expose to peer review.
Applicable to	All organisations.
Inter-agency prescribing	Agreement of prescribing between hospitals and GPs to minimise the cost to the local health community.
Applicable to	All organisations.
Stock disposals	Note and minimise all stock disposals.
Applicable to	All organisations.
Private placements	Increase local capacity to avoid private

	placements, carry out diagnostic justification for use of private sector.
Applicable to	All organisations.
Product standardisation	Standardise products as much as possible across the health economy and increase consignment stock.
Applicable to	All organisations.
Equipment service agreement	Managed services agreement for equipment.
Applicable to	All organisations.
Asset management	Planned asset replacement programme to optimise maintenance costs compared with asset replacement. Regularly test whole life cost repair and maintain or replace.
Applicable to	All organisations.
Asset losses	Asset control minimising losses. Take stock and identify losses and reasons for losses. Improve custody of assets.
Applicable to	All organisations.
Revaluation of assets	Reclassification and revaluation of assets.
Applicable to	All organisations.
Housing association	Housing association deregulation.
Applicable to	All organisations.
Leases	Buy out leases where cost effective to do so.
Applicable to	All organisations.

Corrections	Correct overstatement of opening creditors and provisions.
Applicable to	All organisations.
Year end accruals	Ensure year-end accruals are not overstated.
Applicable to	All organisations.
Capital charges	Correct overstated capital charges.
Applicable to	All organisations.
Depreciation	Depreciation (extend useful life) and consider accounting treatment of capital network in progress.
Applicable to	All organisations.
Capitalisation	Capitalise cost of assets incorrectly allocated to revenue.
Applicable to	All organisations.
Slippage	Use slippage on revenue schemes to offset deficits non-recurrently.
Applicable to	All organisations.
RTA charges	Maximise income from RTA charges.
Applicable to	NHS trusts.
Car parking	Car parking charges.
Applicable to	All organisations.
Charitable support	Promotion of charitable support.

Applicable to	All organisations.
Optimise use of central budgets	Ensure bids are lodged for all available funds that improve productivity and or cost efficiency.
Applicable to	All organisations.
Legal charges	Sale of legal charges over property
Applicable to	All organisations.
Patient income	Patient income.
Applicable to	All organisations.
Other income	Income from public mortuary, overseas visitors and private patients system.
Applicable to	All organisations.
Cat 3 income	Maximise category 3 incomes such as income from post mortem examination.
Applicable to	Mainly NHS trusts.
Advertising and sponsorship	Advertising and sponsorship.
Applicable to	All organisations.
Asset sales	Sell access to under-utilised MRI and other facilities to other service providers and the private sector.
Applicable to	Mainly NHS trusts.
NHS Plus	'NHS Plus' sale of NHS occupational health services to the private sector.
Applicable to	Mainly NHS trusts.

Intellectual property	NHS exploitation of intellectual property. Awaiting legislation.
Applicable to	All organisations.

7. Financial Management Processes, Systems of Internal Control and Capacity

Standing orders and standing financial instructions	PCT SOs and SFIs require the PCT board to satisfy its financial duties to meet its revenue and capital resource limits, cash limit, achieve operational financial balance and full cost recovery by its provider arm. Each board decision incurring new costs should be informed by minuted advice by the Accountable Officer on compliance with statutory duties in general and impact on affordability in particular.
Applicable to	PCTs.
How will it help recovery?	Should stop board agreement or agreement by others to recommendations that breach financial duties by agreeing to incur new costs worsening a forecast deficit.
Compliance	Observation of SOs and SFIs
Validation	No board decisions should be made to increase net revenue costs in the same period that the PCT is forecasting a deficit.
Key milestones to delivery	Board approve SOs and SFIs recommended by the Accountable Officer (Chief Executive).
Key References	DH guidance on SOs and SFIs available on the website.

Standing orders & standing financial instructions	Trust SOs and SFIs require the Trust board to satisfy its financial duties to break even, not exceed the EFL, achieve the CCA and keep capital expenditure within a net capital resource limit. Each board decision incurring new costs should be informed by minuted advice by the Accountable Officer on compliance with statutory duties in general and impact on affordability in particular.
Applicable to	NHS Trusts.
How will it help recovery?	Should stop board agreement or agreement by others to recommendations that breach financial duties by agreeing to incur new costs worsening a forecast deficit.
Evident by	Observation of SOs and SFIs. No board decisions are made to increase net revenue costs in the same period that the Trust is forecasting a deficit.
Reference	DH guidance on SOs and SFIs available on the website.
Budget book	The board confirms through the approval of a 'Budget Book' that the delegated authority to budget holders does not exceed the organisation's total budget, limits budget holders' order limit, and ensures budget holders are held accountable for incurring new costs in excess of budget.
Applicable to	All organisations
How will it help recovery?	Operational managers do not work to budgets that are corporately unaffordable

	and do not commit to new costs without authority.
Evident by	Systems exist that ensure operational budgets do not exceed the corporate budget and budget holders do not commit to new costs without approval. Corporate budgets are not exceeded.
Delegation of authority	Managers have delegated authority to take immediate action upon the detection of cost pressures not detected by risk and sensitivity analysis of cost drivers.
Applicable to	All organisations.
How will it help recovery?	New costs are avoided or minimised.
Integrated planning	The Board agrees to an integrated set of Local Delivery Plans, Capacity Plans, Operational Plans and Recovery Plans, Service Level Agreements, organisational, directorate and departmental budgets.
Applicable to	All organisations.
How will it help recovery?	New activity plans do not incur new costs without approval.
Integrated plans affordable	Integrated Trust/PCT plans and strategies demonstrate that planned performance is deliverable affordably.
Applicable to	All organisations
How will it help recovery?	Managers do not work to unaffordable plans.
Evident by	The board agree plans are deliverable affordably. Plans are supported by service level agreements and valid cost estimates.

Capital investment decisions	Investment decisions are supported by competent economic appraisal and affordability analysis.
Applicable to	All organisations.
How will it help recovery?	Unaffordable developments are avoided.
Control over developments	Any development in clinical practice that has a material resource implication is approved by an appropriate executive clinical committee and the development does not take place until approval is give to the clinical aspects and a budget change is approved by the accountable officer on the recommendation of the Director of Finance. This approval shall be supported by economic appraisal and affordability analysis.
Applicable to	All organisations.
Compliance control	Any material departure to control systems is reported to the board or audit committee.
Applicable to	All organisations.
Management reporting	Monthly reports on service and financial performance are provided at all levels of accountability and are understood by managers accountable for performance.
Applicable to	All organisations.
Benchmark reporting	Budget holders and others accountable for financial performance are regularly advised of their performance compared with benchmark performance of similar organisations, functions and or services.

Applicable to   All organisations.

Budget profiling   Budgets, in year, are profiled using a clear
                                 understanding of cost drivers and the
                                 board is advised of any material changes
                                 to budget profiles.

Applicable to   All organisations.

Sound forecasting   Predictive financial information systems are
                                 sensitive to changes in cost drivers and
                                 deviations from financial profiles. This
                                 enables accurate forecasting of costs and
                                 early detection of performance issues.

Applicable to   All organisations.

Risk management   Risk management systems identify risks to
                                 the achievement of financial targets and
                                 enable the proactive management of risk to
                                 avoid or minimise the impact of risks
                                 being realised.

Applicable to   All organisations.

Clinical risk management   Clinical risk management to reduce
                                 litigation and CNST premium.

Applicable to   All organisations.

How will it help recovery?   Avoid cost, speedier recovery
                                 and mitigation.

8. Other

Advice to the board   At each meeting of the board the executive
                                 report on year to date and full year
                                 projected service and financial
                                 performance. This will also include reports
                                 that reflect indicators of productivity, cost

efficiency and raise issues of inefficiency such as cancellation of theatre sessions.

Applicable to

All organisations. Proposals to improve productivity and save money are implemented. Ensure systems exist that ensure good ideas are presented to the board and agreed ideas are implemented. Implementation of good ideas is evident.

Advice on initiatives

At each meeting of the board the board receives reports from directors accountable for reviewing the findings, advice and directions arising from investigations and studies carried out by the Healthcare Commission, the National Audit Office, the Public Accounts Committee, the Health Select Committee, Public Health Observatories, Royal Colleges and academic reviews, and other appropriate sources of good advice on improving financial health.

Applicable to

All organisations.

Board action

When the board is advised of a predicted deficit or risk of a deficit it directs the Executive to develop a FRP in partnership with other NHS organisations within the local health community. The financial recovery plan to be presented at the following board meeting or sub-committee established to direct financial recovery.

Applicable to

All organisations.

Executive accountability

The individual performance review of the Chief Executive and executive directors will be informed by the delivery of board approved plans including the recovery plan. Executive focus and motivated to deliver key performance requirements.

Applicable to   All organisations.

Management accountability   Clear identification of persons who have accepted and received delegated authority to manage the delivery of service and financial targets.

Applicable to   All organisations.

Personal accountability   Build targets into job description and provide the necessary support to deliver. Budget holders are held accountable for delivering service targets within budget.

Applicable to   All organisations.

Integrated planning and IPR   Performance reporting directly reflects delivery of performance targets by accountable managers. Directly match accountability to performance management - will highlight individuals that need greater support and accelerate recovery.

Applicable to   All organisations.

Consider best practice   The board routinely receives reports on National Audit Office, external and internal audit and clinical audit reports, Audit Commission, prepared to improve service value for money. The board also receives reports prepared to improve service value for money. The board also receives reports on other advice provided by other agencies such as the modernisation agency.

Applicable to   All organisations.

Advice to budget holders on best practice

Effective knowledge management supports the earliest possible detection and adoption at the operational level of best practice to improve value for money.

Applicable to

All organisations.

Management training

Help non-finance specialists understand and apply financial concepts required to maintain financial control.

Applicable to

All organisations.

Notes

Notes